Misfit in Hell To Heaven Expat

Lessons from a Dark Near-Death Experience and How To Avoid Hell in the Afterlife

A Memoir By

M. K. MCDANIEL

www.franklinrose.com

Publisher: Franklin Rose Publishing

ISBN: 978-1-952146-12-1

Library of Congress Control Number: 2020904901

Some names and identifying details have been changed to protect the privacy of individuals.

This book does not deny or promote any religion.

Content Warning: Please be advised that certain portions of this book contain disturbing events that may trigger a reader who has experienced physical and/or sexual trauma.

This book is dedicated to my family, friends, the countless kind souls who continuously supported my transition to a more purposeful life, and to my number one Soul Mate, who inspired me during his life and beyond, and who is saving me a place in heaven.

“This was the power of evil, he thought before drifting off to sleep. Nothing need be actually done to you, just the idea of it, the rumor of it, the sense of the possibility of it. That was enough.”

Once Night Falls by Roland Merullo

“The three most important
words in the
English language:

God, Love and Home.

They are all the same thing.”

The Stupidity Insight by Allen
Johnson Jr.

Table Of Contents

Part III: Hell & Heaven On Earth

Part V: Recovery

Part VI: Lessons

Preview: It Begins

I didn't feel dead, only confused.

Total darkness and absolute silence, my only references.

Not daring to move, I waited.

The blackness morphed into a reddish glow, dragging with it a stinking heat. Acrid fog, muffled moans, and ungodly shrieks.

This can't be good.

Something was staring at me.

Like a blow, a voice thundered, *"Do you know where you are?"*

My mind raced, searching for some rational explanation, but part of me already knew. *"Hell?"* I whispered.

To my horror, the answer was an earsplitting, maniacal laugh.

The evil crept closer as I clamped shaking hands over my ears.

Panic surged in me, triggering the requirement for fight or flight.

Fighting was not an option.

I turned and ran.

Introduction

Accurately verbalizing the ecstasy of heaven and the horror of hell is impossible.

Most people are joyfully attentive as I attempt to share my sense of oneness with God and the treasure of interacting with my deceased friend. But, when inviting that same soul to accompany me on my lengthy sojourn in hell, the experience for my companion shifts.

Following my release from the rehabilitation hospital, I felt compelled to put my extraordinary experiences on paper. The positive and negative memories of living in other realms haunted and depressed me.

I reasoned that by airing my overwhelming feelings, they would fade with the passage of time like a bad dream. Maybe a return to my old life was possible.

It didn't work that way.

Since my prior spiritual structure had produced unsatisfactory results, I continued to search fervently for a better path. At my "final death," I desire a straight shot to God's presence without unpleasant detours.

After countless hours of prayer, introspection, and assistance, I have gradually emerged from my nightmarish cocoon into a lighter space. Still, evil is jealous and relentless, and the haunting continues to this day.

In preparing this written account, I found my current earthly existence to have been greatly influenced by prior relationships over many generations, and thus began the deep dive into my family tree.

With the assistance of a genealogy website along with family memorabilia and stories, I gradually spotted tendencies, such as alcoholism and physical abuse, ingrained in some family groupings and staunchly avoided in others.

Similar challenges appeared in each generation, and I was mesmerized by the myriad ways they were met, some more successfully than others. These challenges even carried over into my life, to my children's lives, and to their offspring.

Conclusions led me to accept my family's flaws and strengths as the overall human condition. Our human nature tends to lean towards negative addictive behavior, but the spiritual component of our universal makeup often seeks redemption.

If this life is a learning experience, as many people who brush up against death claim, and eventually we return to our heavenly home for feedback and encouragement, it puts a different spin on everything we do.

Understanding we are actors in a universal play, with an ultimately happy ending, may give us the hope and courage to forgive our ancestors and encourage our future families to implement change for the better.

PART I:
FAMILY TREE

1

Pilot's Story

My nineteen-year-old future father, an avowed atheist, negotiated a pact with God as he hung upside down in his crashed fighter plane on a Philippines' battlefield in 1942. The first time he shared his story with me was on his ninety-sixth birthday:

"Tacloban airstrip; my good luck ran out. I took a bullet in the oil tank located in front of the cockpit canopy. The windshield quickly covered with hot oil, and I was unable to see directly ahead.

"I opened the cockpit canopy and looked out the side. I noticed one of our own F6F Hellcats had landed ahead of me and was stopped dead in the center of the runway, blocking the landing area.

"With my engine overheating and starting to sputter, I turned to the only other place to land—the sandy beach. As I touched down, my landing gear dug into the sand and the plane tumbled through the air. It came to rest upside down on top of me. My head was buried in the sand, and I was unable to breathe.

"Sensing I was soon doomed to die, I thought, *Lord, get me out of this mess, and I will become a Catholic.*

"Miraculously, the airplane lifted off me, and my head came out of the sand. I gasped for air. Some of our soldiers had left the safety of their 'fox holes' and shifted the tail of the plane so that the cockpit raised above the sand. I grasped my seat belt lever, gave it a tug, and dropped into the arms of my rescuers. I did survive and I did become baptized into the Roman Catholic faith."

Another pilot had contemplated landing on that same beach behind my father's plane. He changed his mind after witnessing my father's aircraft crash and cartwheel three times over the sand before landing upside down. At the time, the pilot assumed Dad had been killed.

These two veterans met at a WWII reunion years later. Dad was surprised to learn of the triple cartwheel, and the other pilot couldn't believe Dad had survived.

Dad's scalp and ear were torn loose in the landing. He fractured three vertebrae and suffered a concussion. The jungle medics stitched his scalp and ear back in place but spared no time for further attention. At the makeshift hospital, Dad met another crash survivor, a pilot being treated for serious burns to both hands and his face.

In addition to suffering ill-treated horrible wounds, my father and his new comrade found themselves stranded on the war-torn beach in the Philippines. Both men attempted to leave the area on a departing Navy vessel but were not allowed to do so without written "orders."

Although injured and in shock, they were simply instructed to return to their base in Hawaii. They carried no identification cards or money and were clad only in ragged, bloodied flight suits.

When I asked Dad how they managed to return to Hawaii, he just smiled and said they "hitched" and boasted they arrived at their appointed base just as their assigned ship pulled into the harbor.

Like most World War II participants, my father never received any assistance with his post-traumatic stress. He, like many others, decided to put his war experiences behind him and wouldn't talk about them to anyone. However, his horrendous memories remain fresh in his psyche decades later.

Dad served a total of thirty years in the Navy before retiring as a captain. At ninety-six, he still suffers the severe back pain that remained with him since his trauma at nineteen. He never complains about it and is still an avid Catholic.

2

A Diseased Branch

Helena and Douglas

My mother, Ann, was born in Kansas City, Missouri and grew up as an only child until she was sixteen. Her mother surprised the family, and herself, with a baby.

Ann's mother, Helena, the favorite child of a doting mother and quiet father, bubbled with joy and personality. She loved parties and people and took great interest in hair styles and the latest fashions. Helena wasn't a deep person, but she was lovable and kind.

In contrast, Ann's father, Douglas, appeared a stern man, one from a large family of many younger brothers. His mother, my great-grandmother, suffered from rheumatoid arthritis and spent most of her later life disfigured and riddled with pain in a wheelchair.

Bleak black and white photographs of his family ooze unhappy faces in distressing circumstances. They appeared unapproachable and wary, and I didn't mind never meeting them.

In those pictures, Douglas stands out as the best dressed of the family, almost jaunty, with hair oiled and parted perfectly, and sporting an enigmatic smile. He aspired to a better life; the one fate dealt him wouldn't do.

After graduating from business school, Douglas transferred to a larger town, determined to increase his chances of launching a successful career. Having received his degree in banking, and earning tuition money working for a bookkeeping service, his resume was sufficient for the times.

A newspaper solicitation for a job as a teller in the new bank in town piqued his interest, and he immediately visited the manager with his resume.

His business-like demeanor and proper attire gave him instant credibility. Instead of hiring him as a teller, they led him to a supervisor's desk, gave him a welcoming smile, and shook hands with him.

His former life became a distant bad memory as he turned his attention to acquiring a socially suitable wife.

Douglas met Helena at a dinner party honoring a visiting dignitary. Chaperoned by her mother, Helena exuded health, charm, and beauty. Douglas deemed she might meet his high standards and began their courtship.

He introduced himself to the ladies and proceeded to charm Helena's mother. A few chaperoned meetings allowed Douglas to subtly study his possible mate. Douglas clinched the deal three months later over cigars and strong coffee in her father's office.

A date set, the announcements were addressed and posted one week later.

Douglas was pleased, and Helena, caught up in the romantic mystery of it all, drifted along in a dreamy fog. Her parents breathed sighs of relief at the promising match.

The wedding photos of Helena and Douglas evoke a feeling of festivity and social correctness. The special events reporter for the local newspaper shamelessly name-dropped the high-society attendees and proffered detailed descriptions of the flowers, gown, and wedding feast.

My mother recently presented me with my grandmother's *Bride's Memory Book* and the *Wedding Guests* booklet, along with pictures and souvenirs of the wedding event. The gala took place in the bank president's mansion, and the well-wishers, plus family members, numbered 101 souls. I counted.

When the bank opened a second branch, Douglas ascended to the status of manager. His outside duties included entertaining prominent and wealthy locals to entice them to bring their plentiful funds to his establishment.

The young couple's social life came of age in the Roaring Twenties and typically involved intemperate drinking. Their lack of experience, coupled with Douglas' drive for success, led to disaster as they crossed the line from social drinkers to functioning alcoholics.

Helena was a happy drunk. Douglas wasn't.

At work, Douglas appeared calm, thoughtful, and professional. With a few hard drinks under his belt, the scene changed abruptly. Rage and brutality took over.

Raised in an environment complicated by a debilitated mother and too many children, Douglas' father's chosen method of securing order and control started with purposefully removing his leather belt and glaring malevolently. His son, Douglas, was too refined for outright beatings; he preferred to punish his family's offenders with a vicious face-targeted slap of his manicured hand.

Their daughter Ann's recollections of her childhood begin when she was old enough to have friends visit her home after school. She never offered reciprocation when asked to come for dinner or to sleep over, for fear that her over-imbibing parents would embarrass her and cause scandalous rumors at school.

She spent as much time as possible away from her home.

Gratefully, in Ann's sophomore year of high school, she applied for, and received, a scholarship to an upscale all-girls academy. Financially unable to live on campus, she commuted the short distance by bus.

Surrounded by happy, wealthy girls from fine families, Ann blossomed. Both beautiful and friendly, she was soon asked to pledge a sorority. Ann felt like Cinderella. She never turned down an invitation to spend a weekend with a friend and never spoke of her family to anyone.

The first time her father attacked her occurred shortly after her enrollment in the young women's academy. His alcohol-muddled mind imagined her out of his control and getting into all sorts of trouble.

The way to stave off this eventuality, he determined, was to follow her up to her bedroom one night, rant into her innocent and startled face about young men's intentions and throw her down the stairs as a warning.

After that event, on the nights she returned home to find her father already drinking, Ann knew to quickly lock her bedroom door after silently climbing her steps to the attic room.

If her father sensed Ann entering the house, he usually left his drinking and staggered down the hall to shout terrible things about her.

"Slut!" he would yell. "Open this door!"

As he beat his fist against her door, her mother would sit shaking at the dinner table, frightened and powerless.

Despite her father's threats, Ann secretly dated young men with successful fathers. Their names featured prominently in the business columns of the newspaper.

Once, a chauffeur came to her friend's house to fetch Ann for an alleged cozy family dinner in a spacious mansion on the golf course. Ann's date was due to inherit an incredible fortune, and he was crazy about her. As their servants deftly served the cook's usual superb fare, his parents and grandmother wondered aloud about her bloodline during the sumptuous repast. Ann didn't offer it was probably 90 proof.

One spring night, Ann and a girlfriend attended a local high school dance on a whim. They danced with nearly every young man in the gymnasium as they laughed and enjoyed the attention.

After a short break, thc band erupted with a tast-paced, popular tune. Ann felt a tap on her shoulder, and as she turned, a stranger held out his hand. Her eyes widened as the tall, handsome young man looked straight into her eyes with a confident, infectious smile. His name was Dean.

Ann and her friends regularly practiced all the latest dance moves in the dorm rooms after classes, and she was an excellent dancer. Although most of the young men they met could fake their way through the newer steps, this fellow danced better than any boy she'd ever met.

For the remainder of the evening, neither desired another partner and only sought to catch their breath between songs. They grinned at each other with shared delight as each new song started up.

Ann never felt so in sync with anyone in her entire life.

As the final song for the evening began, he pulled her close and whispered into her ear, "This will be our song."

It was "At Last."

She was hooked, and so was he.

Unfortunately, he was dirt poor.

3

Grandpa's Dusty Lineage

My paternal grandfather, Henry, was born and raised on a small family farm in the Midwest along with six brothers. This abundance of males proved helpful to his balding father, John, as they share-cropped their small acreage from dawn to dusk.

Henry's mother, Mary Elizabeth, eleven years younger than her husband, was responsible for raising babies, vegetables, and chickens.

In addition, her resume included skills in: cooking, cleaning, washing clothes, canning, pumping water, acting as nurse, feeding wood to the stove for warmth and food preparation, making clothing out of flour sacks, shucking corn, and other fun activities.

If she managed to find some spare time, she picked cotton at the harvest.

With no daughters to help her, my great-grandmother struggled alone for years until a girl named Rachael from the neighboring farm became old enough to come help.

The men folk worked relentlessly, raising cash crops of cotton and corn. Their small percentage of the harvested crops purchased more seed, tools, sugar, and flour. No funds remained for frills.

A family photo of my great grandparents shows them in hand-hewn rockers on a small wooden porch in front of what appears to be a large run-down shack. Neither were smiling, and I don't blame them.

Their clothes appear relatively clean; my great-grandmother's hair is in a tight grey bun, and my great-grandfather's head is covered by a dilapidated hat. Their grim jaws suggest a lack of teeth. I'd guessed them to be in their seventies, but my father told me they were probably in their forties.

4

Rachael's Perspective

My paternal grandmother, Rachael, for whom I was named by my father against my mother's wishes, descended from a family similar to my grandfather Henry's clan.

Her father, William, walked with a slight limp since being kicked by a mule as a young lad. He overcompensated for this disability by becoming the local arm-wrestling champion.

Henry and Rachael's fathers were cousins, both tall and stocky, and their farms adjoined with a meandering creek acting as the property line.

Each set of their parents produced seven living children. Miscarriages and dying babies didn't count much in those days to anyone but the grieving mothers.

Rachael's mom, Edna, bore five sons in quick succession and then rejoiced secretly when two daughters followed. William growled that his cousin's wife gave her husband seven strong sons. Edna knew the poor woman had no female relative to assist her with all her chores and duties and dismissed her husband's disapproval.

Pretty Rachael and her buck-toothed sister, June, learned early on to appear gainfully busy in all their waking hours. To stay under their father's radar required a quiet and compliant demeanor as well as the appearance of earning their keep, or they would share their brothers' belt welts. He still held a grudge they were just daughters, instead of sons.

Their mother patiently taught the young girls all requirements for a safe and predictable present and future, just as her own mother had carefully taught her.

Not only must they learn the obvious basic survival skills required as the wife of a hard-working husband, and future mother of a large brood, but they must learn to read quiet undercurrents and heighten their perceptions. It was well known that many husbands took out their frustrations on an irritating wife.

Their own well-being depended on keeping peace at all costs. There was no place in their strict society for lazy or disrespectful women. They must know their limits and make no demands. Their husbands would expect—no, require—sons from her to keep the farm an asset, not a liability.

If a woman was lucky, Edna cautioned, her husband might appreciate her sometimes, and hopefully, show her some respect. There wasn't time or energy for romantic love and sappy affection in this part of the world, she added.

This scenario never set quite right with Rachael, although June lapped up every word of wisdom her mother spoke in her hushed tones.

Private conversations rarely occurred in this small wooden house with few interior walls, so Rachael and her sister confided in one another while gathering eggs in the hen house or pulling weeds in the garden.

One blistering afternoon, Rachael shared her dream of leaving their dull country life and starting an adventure somewhere else in a world far beyond stinky manure, backbreaking chores, and weather extremes. June hushed her with a finger pressed to her thin lips and looked about in terror for a brother-spy.

When the opportunity arose for Rachael to assist her father's family on the adjoining farm, her excited reply almost cost her the chance. Showing enthusiasm indicated something akin to fun might ensue, so she quickly added a mournful murmur of not wanting to take on extra chores.

Rachael's compliant demeanor shifted the power. She rejoiced inwardly as her father ordered her to assist his cousin's wife, Mary Elizabeth, after church on Sundays until further notice. Rachael's spirits soared at the thought of spending time with a woman other than her mother and intermingling with six boys who weren't her intolerable brothers.

The temporary arrangement became a ritual, and Rachael enjoyed every minute of it.

She felt appreciated for the first time in her life and glowed when the boys teased her gently or complimented her on a supper she took great pains to cook.

Returning to her home late Sunday evenings depressed her, but she lived for Sunday mornings. Years passed as she morphed from a subservient girl into a capable young woman.

My grandpa, Henry, couldn't conceive of a life that didn't entail hard work. When he was of marrying age, the pretty helpmate of his mother, Rachael, looked like an easy choice for a suitable wife.

Henry was remarkably good looking and soft spoken, yet strong of character. Of the seven brothers, Henry knew he appeared the best husband candidate to Rachael.

One Sunday, young Henry called out her name quietly as she made her way to the garden, then surprised her when he pulled a daisy from behind his back and shyly handed it to her.

Rachael gasped in astonishment as blood rushed to her face unbidden. Her fingers trembled as she looked into his brilliant blue eyes and at his wide smile.

Pressing the blossom to her breast, she turned and ran back to the house, suddenly feeling special and grown up.

Rachael felt confused; it seemed as if her life had somehow taken an unexpected turn. That night in bed with June, she attempted to imagine including Henry in her future escape plans.

Since his interest in her had been revealed with the presentation of the flower, Rachael plotted as to how she might wrap Henry around her finger and entice him to alter his future with her.

Henry and Rachael's trip to the altar began with the daisy, progressed with a potted rose, and was agreed upon with Henry's hat-in-hand asking of Rachael's father for her hand in marriage.

Rachael had no real say in the matter other than to nod positively when her father asked gruffly if she would agree. Unspoken was her commitment to change the outcome of their lives to one much different from what others had pre-planned. Rachael's rarely used feminine wiles would prove to be insufficient.

The parents of the prospective bride and groom approved of the family linkage of their adjoining farms. Those precious acres of dirt acted as savings accounts for future generations.

Rachael and Henry's wedding lured relatives from far and near, all bearing gifts of home-made food and hand-stitched finery. Canned goods, kitchen items, and pretty nightgowns came with bows tied around them and overflowed from the porch.

An abandoned temporary structure was transformed into Henry and Rachael's new residence with the assistance of all the males from both families.

Festive food served on precious plates disappeared in minutes even though the women spent hours on their careful preparation. Rachael wore her mother's wedding dress and flowers from Mary Elizabeth's garden in her hair.

Nine months after an unromantic honeymoon event, my father, Dean, was born. With the new baby to care for, Rachael's life seemed on a path to mirror her mother's.

Rachael's cherished dreams of independence and having fun were swapped for serious doubts as Rachael and Henry's baby daughter arrived nine and a half months after their son's birth.

The local midwife offered no sympathy, or relief for her birthing pains, but grimly did the expected and took her wages in hen's eggs and sweet butter.

As the wailing baby, whose sex had disappointed her father, latched onto her mother's swollen breast, Rachael winced uncomfortably.

Tears stung her eyes as Rachael fought to accept an existence with a husband rooted in his seasonally repetitious life, while she was rotting in hellish poverty and monotony.

Laying in the lumpy bed, she envisioned a dreary life of endless pregnancies and crushing workloads. The once-sustaining innocent dreams of her youth seemed more unattainable than ever.

As the cock crowed that hot morning, Rachael refused to waste her one life, and began formulating a new plan.

A year later, with special care not to allow another pregnancy, she broke the mold of countless generations of women in her family. Rachael sought her freedom by announcing her intention to divorce my grandfather, take her children, and move to the city.

After the initial shock wore off, and with Rachael refusing to be swayed, the local pastor's uncle, who once worked for a lawyer, drew up handwritten divorce papers.

Both families insisted the two children be returned to the farm each summer, when they reached the ages of six and seven, to assist with the planting and subsequent labors. Also, Rachael must renounce any claim to either of the farms, or to any animals or farming equipment.

Henry would pay no support of any kind because the divorce wasn't his fault.

Rachael snatched the paper from the mediator and penned her oft-practiced full name slowly and deliberately, relishing the curl of every letter. She did the same for her copy and tucked it into her only purse.

With her head held high, Rachael smiled brightly at the gloomy contingent and strutted smartly from the dreary house.

The enormity of her actions paralleled a large stone thrown into a pond of the future, whose ripples would affect countless lives, including mine.

Her youngest of five brothers, Marvin, reluctantly agreed to drive Rachael and the two confused, whimpering children to town so they might catch a bus. The only person to follow them to the truck was her sister, June, who could only wave solemnly while she stood nearby weeping.

Rachael loaded her scuffed suitcase into the rusted bed of the family truck, hefted her children, Dean and Billie, onto the front seat, and looked straight ahead as they pulled onto the rutted, dusty road and headed expectantly toward a new life.

Having no precedent for a reaction to this sort of event, the two fractured families watched, amazed and silent, as Rachael departed with her two small children.

5

On Their Own

Grandma Rachael

When my father first told me the story of Grandma Rachael's courage, it transmuted to a legend in my mind. I admired her sense of self and determination against all odds.

Over the years, when my own mother felt irritation at my disregard for her "suggestions" on how to manage my life, she would murmur under her breath, "You're just like your grandmother, Rachael."

Instead of feeling the shame my mom wished upon me, I felt pride and a strong sense of my grandma floating beside me, laughing in that throaty voice of hers.

I learned some of the basic facts of Grandma Rachael's search for a new home and of how she came to support her family. My father doesn't speak of those years very often; I only know they were difficult ones for him and his little sister.

Once Dad recalled with a smile of his mother's confidence as she approached one city store owner after another, offering her services for employment. Since most women stayed at home with their children and had working spouses, she was an anomaly and had no prior experience or references.

Rachael's persistence landed her a job in a hardware store. Her knowledge of tools and machinery from her farm years gave her credence. She was a quick learner, reliable, and motivated. The customers liked her gentle cajoling and sought her out when shopping. After several months, she received a promotion and a welcomed raise.

The little family lived in a boarding house operated by a widow who had single-handedly raised her own six children. She was delighted to watch Dean and Billie while Rachael worked.

Dean considered himself the man of the family as he turned five and looked after his shy sibling, Billie, with great care. When the time came to enter school, he stood on a wooden box to iron their clothes and held Billie's hand whenever they ventured outside.

As a youngster, Dean looked for opportunities to earn extra family income. After school, he collected discarded whiskey bottles from gutters and trash bins and returned them to the distilleries for pennies. After proudly handing his mother half his income, he and Billie splurged the remainder of the loot on sweets.

My father recalls moving several times and told me tales of the various characters who shared their meals and living space over the years. Some of the housemothers were kinder than others, he said, but he and his sister always felt safe.

Every summer, when school let out, Dean and Billie boarded a bus with a note pinned to my dad's sweater detailing instructions to his father's farm. The distance was covered in under a day, so no mishaps occurred, and the children found the journey exciting.

They always received a warm welcome from the two families and enjoyed the interaction with a multitude of uncles, aunts, and cousins. Running barefoot to wade in the creek with contemporaries afforded freedom not found in the city. The food was nourishing and plentiful, and they slept well each night after abundant outdoor exercise and fresh air.

At the end of each short summer, as the children boarded the bus to the city, they solemnly entered the first pencil mark on a feed store calendar to count down the days until they returned to that wonderfully alternative universe.

6

Henry's Last Wife

A decent period passed before Henry opened himself up to the possibility of finding another wife.

Henry met Opal, a sweet farm girl from Georgia, at church a year after Rachael's defection. The sad, quiet, and very handsome man caught her eye, and Opal's vivacious and generous nature nurtured his spirit. Although fourteen years younger than he, she fit seamlessly into his wary family.

In the early 1930s, Henry and Opal married in a small ceremony, and their only child, Allen, arrived five years later. The boy, frail and sickly, didn't look like a promising farm hand.

Billie and Dean still arrived every year to pitch in on the chores and grew to love Opal. Her baking was legendary throughout the county and her fried chicken took the blue ribbon every year at the fair.

Unable to produce any more babies, she gathered Billie and Dean under her wings and mothered them like her own offspring.

In the early 1940s, as their acreage gradually eroded to dust and began blowing away, one of

Henry's brothers, Buford, wrote from California and praised the job opportunities there.

In 1946, Henry and Opal loaded everything possible into, and onto, their only vehicle, secured their ten-year old son, Allen, into a rocking chair on top of the heap to keep an eye on everything, and slowly made their way west.

Grandpa found work driving an oversized milk transport truck, and Opal worked in a cannery, eventually becoming a supervisor. Allen attended local schools and after an honorable discharge from the Army, became a type-setter for the local newspaper.

7

Rachael Thrives

Working tirelessly, Grandma Rachael managed to put a little money aside to buy a franchise for a cutting-edge contraption called an Exercycle. She traveled over three states in her territory and spent less time with the children as they grew older. A born horse trader, she excelled in sales and brought in a respectable income.

Rachael never tired of the long hours of driving and the time spent with her customers. She relished the sweet reality of her long-held dream of independence.

As Dean and Billie neared high school, they spent much of their time with friends. This gave Rachael time to socialize, which was an aspect of her life she'd forgone for almost a decade after her divorce.

She was still attractive, in a reckless sort of way, always affable, and had developed a witty sense of humor. Men loved the challenge of her seemingly strong walls of independence and self-control.

Beneath Rachael's bold exterior, a voracious hunger lurked, fueled by her lack of affection as a child, especially from her aloof father.

Any kind word, small gesture of gratitude for her efforts, or warm show of caring for her triggered a magnetic response to the individual offering the nourishment. Her desire to cling to any token of love overcame her need for emotional protection.

Undeniably vulnerable, the charming men she encountered offered her late-night dinners and alcoholic drinks. Unequipped with any social skills, Rachael reasoned to acquire them by learning to smoke cigarettes and drink fancy cocktails.

The smoking bothered her children, but the drinking ruined her life.

As a result of Rachael's lack of judgement while under the influence, the casual dating escalated into affairs, and her embarrassing indiscretions became more frequent.

Dean had no experience with alcoholics in his farm family and found himself unable to stifle her destructive behavior as he attempted to rescue her time and again. Despite his best efforts, Dean eventually despaired of saving his mother from herself.

While Billie and Dean attended high school, Rachael married a nasty-tempered alcoholic they detested. He insisted they call him "Mr. Jackson" and demanded their respect for himself and their deteriorating mother. Their home life became intolerable.

8

Independence Day

Unable to interact sanely with his alcoholic mother and her arrogant husband, Dean left home.

His best friend, Art, offered to put him up temporarily. After a week or so, the parents of his friend took pity on him and offered Dean their one-car garage/storage shed to live in until he graduated.

Dean found a part-time job. He paid a bit toward the room and board, but there remained little left over.

Art's brother had joined the Army and left all his civilian clothes behind. Dean and the brother were both tall and very thin, and Art's parents lent Dean his clothes.

One spring night, dressed in borrowed clothes, Dean attended his high school dance with a friend and met the love of his life.

Their young relationship blossomed into a great love story.

9

Learning To Trust

Following Ann outside after a fairytale evening, Dean boldly asked for her phone number. She didn't hesitate to write her best friend's number on a scrap of paper and tucked it into his shirt pocket. They nervously searched for goodnight words as their friends pulled them in opposite directions.

When Dean phoned her later that evening at her friend's house, there ensued a minor confusion when Dean thought he was talking to Ann but was speaking to her friend.

Grabbing the phone when she realized it was Dean, Ann put off an explanation for the mix-up, saying they needed to speak about it in person. They hastened to set a time and place to do so.

At a malt shop near the high school campus, two teenagers sought a private table for their first date.

Each had secrets. Both required secrecies to continue living that life, lest their carefully constructed personas fall apart and expose them for the losers they thought they were.

Dare they take the chance of exposure based on one fun night of dancing?

Dean deposited two cokes onto their small corner table where Ann sat, devoid of the confident charm she exhibited freely in their initial encounter.

"Tell me about yourself," Dean prodded cautiously.

Ann attempted to speak but only moved her head quickly from side to side as if wanting to shake something loose from her brain. When she looked up, tears brimming in her gentle eyes, his heart began to break.

As Dean's warm compassion washed over her, it produced a tidal wave of grief. His kindness served as a stark contrast to the violent reactions of her own father.

He gently laid his hand over hers and patted it, saying, "It'll be OK."

Ann wanted with all her heart to believe him.

To facilitate a growing trust, they agreed to reveal themselves slowly, making a game of sharing one secret each per meeting.

With the cautious unveiling of myriad ghostly memories, they expressed shock at the similarities of their bleak childhoods. Although the situations were wildly different, the underlying drama and conflicts induced similar cocooning results and the fervent desire to enjoy happier and more orderly lives.

The relationship snowballed as they gained confidence by sharing painful disclosures. Neither offered judgement, only empathy and sympathy, and their need for each other grew.

Ann and Dean found it increasingly difficult to end their meetings.

They experienced their first kiss following a particularly difficult afternoon. As they relished a now-familiar hug, Ann and Dean instinctively knew they could never say goodbye again, only, "See you soon."

Although they were aware of the rumblings of war, they couldn't begin to understand the personal implications looming in their near future. For now, they were dreaming out loud of someday being together on a permanent basis, when they were older.

Fate did not respect their dreams, or those of anyone else in those times, and war was declared only a month after Dean graduated from high school. He was eighteen, and Ann was sixteen.

Dean could choose to wait, and be called up by the draft, or enlist in the service. His lifetime of making decisions for himself, and his sister, gave him confidence, instead of the confusion and fear many of his buddies experienced.

Dean reviewed information concerning an upcoming U.S. Navy's pilot training program and inquired about qualifications. He imagined the exhilarating freedom of flying an airplane, and this freedom felt heavenly to a previously dirt-bound farm boy.

Flying afforded him the ability to transcend foxholes and forego the necessity of shooting people face to face, an idea that turned his stomach.

After Dean passed his exams in the Civilian Pilot Training Program, he moved to the next level of training in a nearby state for two months.

Orders to attend the Naval Flight Training school, and his commission in the United States Navy, arrived as he turned nineteen years old.

During Dean's rapid ascent to a career, Ann suffered in his absence, afraid his new life could eventually exclude hers. She curtailed her social scene and only associated with her female friends.

Not much of a student to begin with, her interest in school barely kept her grades at a passing level. Nothing improved in her rotten home life. She cried into her pillow nightly and lived for Dean's letters.

At the arrival of the orders to present himself at a Naval station in California, Dean felt conflicted. He knew this opportunity would transform him in ways he could only imagine, and his world would finally be orderly and secure.

On the opposite side of the scale awaited a woman who made him feel loved and worthy of love. He dared not imagine his life without her.

Dean and Ann agreed to meet at their malt shop.

She had taken great care with her makeup and dress. He fought to keep his heart in his chest. Dean saw through her calm exterior, into her desperate soul. As he gently took her hands across the table, she stopped breathing.

"I've got to be in California in ten days…" he began.

Unable to hear another word, Ann attempted to keep her composure in the public place, but a sob escaped nonetheless as she cried out, "Dean, don't leave me!"

She yanked her hands from his and covered her eyes. He begged her to look at him, but she shook her head.

"Please, Ann, look at me," Dean pleaded.

Reluctantly, she withdrew her hands, intending to glare at him mercilessly, but gasped wide-eyed instead as she beheld the simple golden ring between his fingers.

10

Unconventional Wedding

Ann and Dean Cutting Their Wedding Cake

Time blurred as the reality of their situation necessitated life-altering decisions.

Ann and Dean had no experience with planning a wedding, finding passage to an unknown area, or the funds to accomplish these events, yet together they felt invincible.

The following day, Ann sought to tap her mother's social skills while her father worked at the office, uninformed of the situation.

Helena purchased an appropriate suit for Ann, and she donated a suitcase from her closet. Together they chose Ann's finest clothes for her new life as a Navy wife and cherished their closest time together ever as mother and daughter.

After telephoning the courthouse, Dean discovered the legal age for marriage in their state was twenty-one. In the bordering state, they could marry if each had a parent to co-sign. They planned to ask Ann's mother first, then Dean's. If the mothers refused, the fathers were not a viable Plan B.

The next day, at the crack of noon, Helena left her bed to meet with Ann and Dean in her kitchen. She took three aspirin as the couple unfurled their wedding plans.

Since Ann's father would be attending a bank dinner meeting that evening, they decided to implement their plan at five o'clock.

Helena began fussing over what to wear, refrained from her usual five o'clock tiddly for once, and awaited their arrival.

Grandma Rachael, more than a bit hungover when approached, enthusiastically counted herself in, lauding their adventurous spirits, and kissed them both soundly.

Rachael offered to drive the getaway car. Dean had never witnessed this playful side of his mother before and smiled encouragingly.

At the appointed time, Ann's mother, wearing white gloves and a stylish hat, formally introduced herself to Dean's mother, who was clad in trousers and matching jacket. The wedding party piled into Rachael's well-used station wagon, laughing at the tight fit.

Rachael startled her co-conspirators when she erupted into a hearty *Yeee haaa* as she floored her trusty steed. The rest of the merrymakers held on for dear life as they headed east.

Helena tittered and Rachael cackled as the blushing bride chastely kissed her handsome husband after the "I do's." The disparate women would never be Friends of Bill W., but they shared a shiny dream of their children attaining a stable life and marriage, something that had been unattainable for them.

To this day, over seventy-six years later, my parents remember the facts of this event differently. Dad remains vague when asked whether or not he lied about their ages, which triggers Mom's doubt of having been legally married.

That they obtained a marriage certificate and still love each other are the only certainties since all the other witnesses took the evidence to their graves.

PART II

THE “NEW KID” EVOLUTION

11

Instant Grown-Ups

Ann and Dean barely contained themselves as they struggled to appear like a normal married couple traveling across the country. They felt akin to children playing house or actors in a movie.

They sought to stave off the giggles when fellow passengers inquired about the obvious honeymooners, who blushed and lowered their eyes when referred to as Mr. and Mrs.

Finding quarters near the Navy base during the war involved following rumors of an empty living space, only to find ten or more other people bartering for the same small room in some local's residence.

Their first home was a screened-in porch attached to a small duplex, with a mattress for a bed and an old dresser for their clothes. Thanking God for the mild San Diego weather, they imagined themselves camping as they shared a single bathroom with six other boarders.

Learning to play bridge with a couple renting a small room in the house offered them entry into a new social circle. The foursome became addicted and started their first game at breakfast. The men came home at lunch for a few hands, and they resumed playing after dinner. The company and banter offered cheap entertainment and forged a lasting friendship.

The fun ceased abruptly when my father's orders for active duty finally arrived.

Dean looked forward to finally using his piloting skills and fighting for his country as Ann prayed unceasingly to a God she knew only casually.

Months dragged on after Dean deployed, and one day Ann received the news her prayers hadn't prevented.

Her husband's plane had crashed in the Philippines, but somehow, he made his way to Hawaii, where he would require hospitalization for an undetermined amount of time for undisclosed injuries. She was heartsick and terribly frightened.

Letters were the only way to communicate with Dean, and the war made it next to impossible for timely delivery. Sometimes the letters weren't delivered at all.

The only thing for her to do was wait, feeling much older than her seventeen years.

12

Starting Anew

After the war ended and my father recovered enough to travel, he was released from active duty. My parents reluctantly traded the bliss of living in California for a return to the seasonally challenged Midwest.

Dad found uninteresting gainful employment and attended college via the GI Bill. Housing was scarce, but they secured a small two-bedroom apartment on the third floor of a large apartment complex.

My mom became pregnant with me, and two years later, my sister, Lynn, joined our family. Residing on the third floor without an elevator offered plentiful exercise opportunities to my parents as they carried prams, groceries, and babies up and down the multitude of stairs.

On hot, humid summer nights, my parents would drag their double mattress through the kitchen onto the small iron balcony, attempting to seek a cooler spot to sleep.

They relied on frugal spending to allow occasional treats. Never abandoning the necessity for fun and adventure, our family regularly caught a streetcar and rode up and down the line, licking ice cream cones with the wind blowing in our hair.

13

More Changes

Lynn, Junior, and Me

When I was about five, Dad returned to active duty as an officer in the Navy and was transferred to the northern East Coast for four years. I remember fantastic drifts of snow in our front yard that Dad carved into ice caves.

My younger brother, dubbed Junior, was born there. The first thing one would notice about my baby brother were his huge brown eyes and long lashes. He initially appeared shy, but as he warmed to someone, Junior the Entertainer emerged.

He never walked, only ran full bore. Junior's smiling face beamed as he climbed furniture, large rocks in the yard, or small trees. His energy was boundless, and he shrugged off injuries with only a tear or two.

Much to my parents' alarm, Junior began stepping on bees in his bare feet for attention before he was three. He developed a severe bee sting allergy, causing him to require an antidote injection with each future sting. This subtle warning went unheeded.

My mother dubbed him "a handful" and told me he was "my fault."

To this day she tells the story of when I was five: *We were Catholics and used the rhythm method to prevent unwanted pregnancy. I kept a calendar in my top drawer and marked an "X" on every "safe day" of the month.*

After a night at a cocktail party, Dean was feeling frisky, and I checked my calendar to find an X on that day.

Time passed, and I started feeling queasy one morning. We had not wanted any more children, so I frantically found my calendar and looked closely. There were three extra X's in a different shade of pencil following my own.

She always stares at me pointedly for the punchline of her story, for in addition to marking the three X's, I had signed my name in kindergarten text at the bottom.

Thus, my brother was "my fault."

14

Meeting My Grandparents

My mom hadn't seen her mother since the wedding. With three unmet grandchildren so far away, my grandmother's letters begged for a visit. After much deliberation, my parents arranged for my mother and me to take a train from the East Coast to the Midwest. My father took vacation time to watch my brother and sister.

As I recall, and my mother confirms, after taking a taxi from the train station, we knocked on the door at her family home and received a warm welcome from my grandmother. Most of my friends had relatives of all ages, and I was understandably excited to finally meet some of mine.

After chatting in the kitchen with my sweet grandmother, my mom asked if her father was home. My grandmother seemed embarrassed to tell us that he was sitting in the living room, reading a paper. He hadn't bothered to come in to greet us, although he knew we had arrived.

My mother rose from her chair and led me by the hand into their living room, where a distinguished man sat in an overstuffed chair, holding a newspaper in front of his face.

After a few seconds, my mother grasped my hand tighter, cleared her throat, and said in a shaking voice: “Dad, this is your granddaughter, Rachael.”

Wearing my best dress and new shoes, a floppy ribbon in my shiny hair, and the biggest smile I could muster, I waited.

The man didn’t stir except to change the page of the paper.

“Dad!” my mother repeated in an impatient voice.

My grandfather slowly lowered the newspaper and stared at me for all of three seconds, then silently returned the paper to cover his face.

I squealed in alarm when my mother’s hand yanked me backward and out of the room. Pulling me too quickly into the kitchen, my furious mother dropped my hand and reached for her coat and hat.

My grandmother covered her face, and I felt frightened and confused as I observed both women crying. *What had ruined our supposedly wonderful visit and turned it into a nightmare?*

The women clung desperately to one another as my grandmother kept repeating, “I’m so sorry. I’m so sorry.”

As Grandma knelt to hug and kiss me, I felt numb.

My mom grabbed her sole suitcase, handed me my favorite baby doll, and slammed the door as we left.

After frenetic haggling with a railroad employee, my mom and I chugged homeward. She sat as still as a statue most of the way as I stared blankly out the window. After her tears dried, I glimpsed a determined, haunted look come into her eyes. We never saw my grandfather again.

The incident was finally discussed when I became an adult, and after I unearthed a picture of my grandfather in a storage box. I asked my mother what happened the day of our visit, and whatever became of him, and she replied dully he had died of liver disease at the age of forty-five due to alcoholism. She alluded briefly to his drunken rants and his physical abuse in a small voice but never filled in the blanks.

My father had saved her, she said, by marrying her when he was called up for active duty in the war.

My dad solemnly added: "I couldn't leave her there with him."

My heart went out for the innocent young woman who had suffered so much and still did her utmost to provide my siblings and me with a childhood full of love and laughter, security and faith. Small in stature but lion-hearted, she is well known in the community as a generous and loving person.

That one visit I experienced with my maternal grandfather left a scar on my soul and caused me to wonder for many years what was so wrong with me that he wouldn't even say hello. I now know rationally of his faults and addiction, but the child in me still feels sad and hurt.

My mother never forgave him for the humiliating trauma, the years of abuse she and her mother suffered at his hands while drunk, or his arrogant silences when sober.

I hope we can sort it all out when I see him in the Afterlife.

15

The "New Kid"

My father's next tour of duty was to the Washington, D.C. area and lasted less than three years. Our housing development perched on the edge of a miniature forest. I spent many hours with Nancy Drew and The Hardy Boys in a rustic treehouse my father built for me.

When I pleaded for a pet, my father told me I could have anything I could capture. A snapping turtle, a praying mantis, a tree frog, a baby robin, and a delicate butterfly took turns being my friends.

I acquired a disturbing nickname on the first day I attended the local elementary school. I was dubbed the "new kid." Small for my age and shy, I became a target for bullies. My survival depended upon adopting a stronger persona and acquiring an ally.

Conjuring up an invisible, younger version of Jesus to be my companion and protector proved effective. When He and I played tag on the playground, I talked to Him out loud. I even heard His Voice answering me, and we had extensive conversations. The other children left me alone, probably thinking I was crazy. I believed He protected me.

As the childhood days passed, my brother seemed to escalate in his need for attention. Although my dad spent time with him, when possible, teaching him to fly a kite or ride a bicycle, his long hours on the job left us little quality time with our father.

My sister and I tried to include Junior in our games, but he soon tired of dolls and dress up and found a neighbor's little girl to be his pal. Unfortunately, their play included lighting matches.

When both four-year-old children were caught playing in the woods with their newfound entertainment, the punishment was swift and painful.

I took to the woods to outrun my brother's cries at the slap of the belt.

Looking back, I guess my brother's need for attention overshadowed his fear of reprisal. Junior's transgressions accelerated as he grew older. His addictive behavior for danger would destroy him.

16

School Days

I attended parochial (Catholic) schools from first grade into college, except for three days in fifth grade, when I ended up in public school.

Upon arrival to yet another new town, my sister and brother found space in the crowded Catholic school, but since there was no room in my grade at the time, my parents placed my name on a long waiting list. I was temporarily enrolled in the public elementary school.

My brief incarceration in that establishment offered me a shock at having the kid behind me ask to cheat off my paper, another child eating an entire crayon before lunch, multiple students sassing the teacher, and other bizarre and unacceptable behaviors. I had never witnessed any classroom disturbance in the nun's territory without severe consequences ensuing. I was scandalized!

At my telling of these transgressions, my parents were horrified. I was rushed to the top of the enrollment list when my mother stormed St. Perpetua's admittance office and demanded rescue of her babe from such debauchery.

17

Perfect Family

I grew up unaware of my parents' backgrounds and their dedicated goal of constructing a perfect family. They had learned individually that the key to survival was to look past woefully imperfect circumstances and instead endeavor to create stable and plentiful futures.

My grandmothers, my mother, and I shared the experience of having a father who didn't know how to love a daughter, but my mother found a devoted partner in Dad. They became an inseparable team, and we children revolved as moons to their planet.

Their shared dream featured a family unit striving for quiet serenity and pleasant interactions. Adequate time for fun and family vacations, elaborate Christmas celebrations, and nightly dinner conversations featuring healthy food would be the predictable norm.

There would be no alcohol.

In reviewing pictures of my childhood holidays, I noted my sister and myself in matching frilly dresses, white gloves, lace-topped socks, and hats secured with elastic under the chin.

My brother was pictured in short pants, skinned knees, and shirts that wouldn't stay tucked in. We were always smiling for Dad as he recorded every happy event.

Unfortunately, these perfect pictures required a lot of rules to keep the wheels on the wagon. Close supervision of our friends, early curfews, specific times for meals, homework, and bedtimes all seemed contrived and confining to me and my siblings. We didn't understand the need for such predictable activities and suffocating control. We yearned for our comrades' freedoms.

Most of our buddies left home in the morning on school days, walked to school, and then walked home. Frequently they dawdled along the way and caught frogs in a stream, made a treehouse in one of their yards, or played in each other's homes. If they were really lucky, homemade cookies were provided.

Driven to and from school by my mother, my siblings and I felt left out. When we objected, my parents complained how ungrateful we were, because their parents never took them anywhere. They just didn't get it. We hated hurting their feelings, and guilt was added to our consciences.

My father worked long hours, and when he came home to us at dinnertime, my mother greeted him with a kiss, an orderly and clean home, and a beautiful meal.

My siblings and I knew not to squabble at dinner, to always use our table manners, and to eat quietly. We listened as my mother gently probed my father for his day's activities, and he answered cheerfully when she shared hers. Dad would ask us about our days, but mostly to be polite.

With the completion of our meal, we children slipped from our chairs to do homework or play quietly in our rooms. My parents sat in the living room and chatted after Dad changed into more comfortable clothing.

When we moved to the Midwest, Dad transformed the basement into an entertainment room; the television resided there for the children to enjoy, plus gave the adults a quiet space upstairs.

As we grew older, the confining rules still applied, even multiplied, and began to chafe uncomfortably as I entered high school.

Throughout the years, my visiting friends would express envy of our young parents and the beautifully perfect environment. They even offered to trade parents with me.

I always accepted, but no transfer ever transpired.

18

Midwest Homecoming

My parents were overjoyed when my father's transfer to the Midwest was announced. My mother was born there, and my siblings and I occasionally heard stories of her and Dad meeting as teenagers at their high school dance.

The memory of my second visit with my maternal grandmother, Helena, was encouraging at first. When we arrived, she greeted us with the same warmth and love that I had felt at our first meeting.

My mom's father, Douglas, had passed away about a year before, and now Grandma had a new husband named Victor; a friend of the family, I was told. The adults exchanged meaningful looks that I couldn't translate.

Since Victor was at work that day, we only visited with my grandmother and Uncle Kenny, who was only four years older than I was. My mother was sixteen when he was born, and she had married and moved out soon after Uncle Kenny's birth.

As my mom and Uncle Kenny met as adults for the first time, they struggled to find common ground and a basis for interacting.

We had arrived with our terrier puppy, Skippy. She specialized in escaping from the house and loved having us run about breathlessly trying to catch her. Within a half hour of our family reunion, my uncle opened the front door to bring in fresh air, and the dog dashed out the door into the busy street.

Before we had the chance to pursue her, we heard tires screeching and an ominous thud. As a group, we gathered at the curb to cry out as our puppy lay mortally injured. My father, who swore to hate dogs, lifted her broken, bleeding body and placed it to his chest.

Accepting car keys from my mother, he carefully placed the wounded animal in the front seat next to him and sped off to a veterinarian's office. He came back without her, informing us that nothing could have been done to return her to a healthy life.

We all mourned deeply, but my sixteen-year-old uncle was stricken with remorse at his accidental involvement with the tragedy. Uncle Kenny, a gentle giant of a teenager, suffered more than the rest of our family.

The day's unpleasant surprise, however, would pale in comparison to the one that soon followed.

19

Unimaginable Tragedy

Shortly after settling into our new home, my maternal grandmother and her new husband perished when a fire erupted in their apartment. Uncle Kenny, who was out working his paper route, returned home to find it in flames.

In a deep sleep after a typical night of overindulging in alcohol, my grandmother and her new husband were unaware of their electric blanket shorting out and catching fire.

By the time my grandmother awoke, and unsuccessfully attempted to rouse her husband, acrid smoke filled the small apartment. She managed to make it to the front door before she succumbed.

Minutes later, my young uncle fumbled with his door key and shouted for his mother inside the inferno. When the lock disengaged, he pushed with all his might, but the door barely moved. His mother's limp body on the other side prevented his entry. As the smoke poured out of the unit, the firemen pulled Uncle Kenny to safety despite his frantic pleas to assist.

The neighbors evacuated in panic. There was nothing to be done except to keep the fire from spreading. Uncle Kenny sat at the curb, crying and coughing, until my father came for him. We welcomed him into our family, but the situation was awkward and unsettling for all of us.

Since Uncle Kenny had been raised by alcoholic parents and learned at a young age to take care of himself, my parents' strict rules and regulations seemed offensive and unnecessary from Uncle Kenny's point of view.

Increased stress and raised voices disrupted my parents' orderly haven. Uncle Kenny's poor school grades, broken curfews, and excessive drinking surfaced emotions my parents hoped to keep safely locked in their pasts.

After graduation, Uncle Kenny joined the Marines with my father's blessing. Bad luck continued to follow him throughout his short life.

Uncle Kenny married and divorced three times. The highlight of such endeavors was James, his only child by his third wife, Carol. When their son was a baby, Carol asked for a divorce and took their son back to her hometown in another state.

Although James was a cousin of mine, we only met on one brief occasion as adults when he stopped by to inform us of his imminent deployment to Afghanistan. James and our family have not kept in touch.

Uncle Kenny lived in our seaside town for many years as a police officer, but between long hours on the job and his hectic personal relationships, we only saw him at holidays. His drinking problem increased, and an accident on the job caused him to retire early.

After a lifetime of alcoholism and smoking, my Uncle Kenny died of emphysema at the age of fifty-four.

In his final year, I visited him every Sunday at his convalescent hospital for a dominos game, which he always won. We shared tacos and popcorn I'd bring, our favorite foods. He was one of my closest relatives, but we never had much quality time together.

We caught up to date on our separate adult lives following his brief living arrangement with us and laughed as we recalled how he would babysit me and my siblings. All four of us still recall Uncle Kenny melting an entire stick of butter to mix with the slightly burnt popcorn he fed us for dinner one night.

Uncle Kenny had died once already from his illness, had a life-changing experience, returned to make amends, and became baptized as a Catholic before returning to heaven for his final time.

His Near-Death Experience occurred in a convalescent home after a breathing emergency resulted in his temporary demise.

My parents, contacted by phone of his impending death, drove swiftly to the facility and raced to his room to find his still body with a sheet pulled over his head. A nurse entered the room as they reacted with alarm to his sudden death and offered condolences.

Sitting on either side of Uncle Kenny, my mother began to cry for her brother, and my father bowed his head to pray.

Suddenly, Uncle Kenny shot up to a sitting position, the sheet slipped from his face, and he exclaimed, "What's going on here?"

My mother leapt screaming from her chair, and my dad grabbed his heart in surprise and shock.

Uncle Kenny demanded to know why they were there, but neither of my bug-eyed parents could utter a sound.

A nurse entered the room at the commotion and shrieked unprofessionally. Getting ahold of herself, she marched to Uncle Kenny's bedside, grabbed his wrist, and checked her timepiece.

"I'm calling your doctor, young man," she said, and eased him back onto the bed.

After much ado, Uncle Kenny was pronounced not dead, much to his relief.

As the story unfolded from Uncle Kenny's point of view, it appeared that he experienced a blackout of sorts, awoke in a realm of incredibly bright light, and found himself talking to Jesus. Since Uncle Kenny wasn't a religious sort, he felt privileged at making the acquaintance.

While they chatted, persons appearing to be his deceased parents diverted Uncle Kenny's attention and asked him to follow them. When Uncle Kenny turned to ask Jesus' opinion, He had disappeared.

Uncle Kenny curiously inquired why he should follow as he peered around for his former companion.

Hearing my father's voice, he whirled to find my parents with outstretched arms, welcoming him to follow them. Understandably, Uncle Kenny felt something wasn't quite right.

Refusing to move, he stared in horror as my supposed parents melted, then emerged as demons, howling and grasping at him with razor claws. Their cries, blood-curdling and distinctive, caused him to pivot and run.

The next thing he knew, a sheet was over his face, and he heard my mother crying.

The staff offered no opinion on the matter, only sought to move him to a bed in the recovery room and eventually to a permanent, semi-private one.

Thus began my weekly pilgrimage to my other-worldly uncle.

Uncle Kenny never missed a segment of *Touched by an Angel*, his favorite television show. He tried to explain to me how the director of the show showed the angel's aura perfectly, just like Jesus', and bet the man had been to heaven too.

Eventually, he shared his total otherworldly experience with me, adding that he believed the demons would eventually claim him unless he made amends and learned more about Jesus. He requested a priest to visit him, took religious education lessons, and became a baptized Catholic.

Uncle Kenny received a welcome visitor from his teenage past. Linda, his high school sweetheart, learned of his whereabouts and his brush with death. She also knew the doctor predicted his permanent death within the coming year.

As I learned from her later, she became pregnant with Uncle Kenny's child shortly after their high school graduation, and she didn't realize she was expecting a child until after Uncle Kenny left for his tour in Korea.

In a panic, knowing that Kenny wasn't interested in marrying her anymore, she accepted the kind proposal of a man who had loved her secretly for years. They raised Kenny's little girl as their own.

Shocked at first, Uncle Kenny felt gratitude at her husband's acceptance of his child. He and Linda spent many hours rekindling their friendship and catching up on his daughter's life. They agreed meeting the young lady now would unnecessarily complicate her life, especially since Uncle Kenny's life expectancy was dwindling.

Uncle Kenny's decline escalated, and a few months later, he passed away quietly amid family and friends.

Many times, he expressed to me his fervent desire to return home and finish his conversation with Jesus. I felt happy for him.

20

Social Snafus

Four years in the Midwest ushered my entry into middle school as the perennial "new kid," tornado alarms that sent us scurrying to the basement, humid summers exploding with thunderstorms, and my first true love.

One more memorable situation occurred. In sixth grade, I thought I killed someone. Accidentally, of course, and only my best friend witnessed the event.

That year the middle school sponsored a Fair Day in May in the gym. They provided games and food booths, bobbing for apples, lassoing barrels, and more. Each of the large classes were afforded an hour and a half, including lunchtime for some, to enjoy the spectacle.

My best girlfriend, Margie, and I perused the glorious scene in our uniformed ensembles and deliberated as to which of the games we might try with our limited funds. Some offered prizes, and others didn't.

I held my friend's cotton candy as she tossed three darts at multicolored balloons on a large wooden board. Margie almost won a package of hair ribbons, and I mourned aloud with her at the loss since she loved adorning her long, blonde hair.

When I handed her my candied apple and accepted three darts from a cute eighth grade boy, I blushed when he smiled at me. He backed out of my throwing range as I shut one eye and aimed at the balloons. I tossed my first dart with vigor.

Just then, for some unknown reason, the boy lunged in front of the board to cross to the other side.

Thump!

The cute eighth grader with the nice smile grabbed his chest and cried out in surprise. He looked at his punctured sweater, and then at me.

Margie shrieked as I dropped my remaining darts to the counter, grabbed my candied apple from her trembling hand, and whispered frantically, "RUN!"

We fluctuated between hysterical tears and uncontrollable giggles of shock as we hid in a dark coat closet near the girl's bathroom. When we finally heard the bell ending our grade's fair session, we slipped back into the hall.

I don't know how we managed to keep it together as we walked like zombies to our final class for the day, purposefully avoiding eye contact with one another.

As I climbed into my mother's car after school on that fateful afternoon, I felt my life was ruined. Although Margie and I swore never to tell a soul of the horrid accident, my conscience screamed, "Murderer!"

Visions of eternal damnation in a carnival hell filled my thoughts. I imagined gleeful demons attacking me with torrid darts for all eternity. The priests and nuns scripted such punishments for telling lies or using improper language, but what happened to murderers?

Fortunately, my mother had the power to read my thoughts and when my siblings settled into their rooms, she put her hand on my shoulder and bent down to investigate my clouded expression.

"Did something happen today, honey?" she asked.

Keeping my head down, my eyes looked up into her loving face.

"I think I killed somebody!" I sobbed and threw my thin arms around her neck. "Please don't tell Dad."

"Well, that's something out of the ordinary." she gently replied. "I'm sure we can straighten this all out, and I do believe your father would prefer to be involved in the process, Rach."

After three freshly baked chocolate chip cookies, my spirits improved, and I found the courage to fill my mother in on the sordid details. She listened attentively, but she seemed to take the news a bit calmly, considering my possible life-sentence in the local penitentiary.

Mom encouraged me to start on my homework, and I left her side with a sigh. Dad usually arrived home for dinner around 5:30 p.m., and I felt conflicted about sharing the tragedy with him.

Memories of the punishing belt used on my brother made me feel nauseous with fear. The demons in my imagination seemed less worrisome than a disappointed and angry father.

In the meantime, my mother secretly telephoned the school office and inquired if the fundraising carnival had been a success and if any problems had arisen.

The secretary reported the event had raised better than expected revenue and all went relatively smoothly. The school intended to repeat the carnival the following year but decided to replace the dart and balloon booth with cotton candy instead.

After her call, and before Dad showed up, Mom opened the door to my room and smiled at me. "I just contacted the school, and no murders occurred at the carnival today. They've decided to replace the dart game with cotton candy next year. Your guardian angel worked overtime today! I'd say a prayer of thanks if I were you."

I dropped to my knees and began to pray but looked up quickly and asked my mother if Dad needed to know what happened at the carnival.

"What carnival?" She smiled and pulled the door closed.

Dad didn't pay attention to things like that, but I knew God did.

I continued praying.

Another traumatic event happened to me in seventh grade, just before first period English. My supposed two best friends asked me to settle a bet between them. One insisted I could fit into a hall locker, and the other said I couldn't. They asked me to prove which one of them was right, to settle the bet.

Innocently, I entered the cramped locker and felt the door slam shut on my twisted body. I froze as their laughter filtered through the slatted metal door. When their footsteps receded down the hall toward our classroom, I got my first taste of claustrophobia. It would not be my last.

Not wanting to be a poor sport, and inexplicably trusting at least one of my friends to take pity on me, I waited until my leg started cramping, then began to yell for help.

Banging my head on the locker door, I paused as a key turned the lock and the door swung open.

The largest, sternest-looking nun in the world eyed me suspiciously and demanded to know why I deliberately shut myself in the locker. She was a new addition to the teaching staff, and I didn't want to appear disrespectful, so I avoided eye contact and whispered, "I'm sorry, Sister."

Swinging the door wider, she eyed me as I untangled myself and attempted to stand erect. After regaining my balance, I bolted down the hall.

Apologizing profusely to my white-habited English teacher for my inexcusable tardiness, my eyes swept the room and beheld a sea of smirking faces.

I hated junior high school.

21

Grandma Rachael

I had seen pictures of myself as a toddler with my namesake, Grandma Rachael, but because of her alcoholism, she and my mother did not get along.

In the photos, Grandma looked on lovingly as I stood in diapers, wearing her high heels and one of her many fancy hats. Another photo features her laughing as her cocker spaniel tugs on my dolly as I attempt to swat him away.

The summer before I started eighth grade, a girlfriend came for a sleepover during one of Grandma Rachael's infrequent visits. My friend and I answered the doorbell, just before our bedtime, to find a strange man with his arm around my grandmother.

Her faithful old-fashioned hat askew, she laughed loudly and greeted us with a flourish, nearly slipping to the ground before the strange man broke her fall.

My friend and I looked on curiously as my mother stomped down the hall, moved us aside, and thanked the taxi driver with a push of bills into his free hand.

My dad arrived in time to accept his limp mother, receive a scathing look from his wife, and to order my friend and me to bed.

The next morning, Grandma Rachael had disappeared.

When questioned, my mother told me succinctly that Grandma was ill and needed to return to her own home. After that, I worried each time I caught a cold or a childhood disease, for fear my mother would just send me away like she did Grandma Rachael.

22

Another Family Reunion

Upon landing in the Golden State, my father took us to be introduced to his long-lost father, Henry, his wonderful second wife, Opal, and their son, Allen, who was ten years my senior.

Their fifty-year-old tract home off the city's main street boasted fruit trees, pampered flowers, and a truck garden in the backyard.

A concrete canal hiding behind the backyard fence ran hither and yon throughout the area, providing life-giving water to crops on countless rural farms.

My siblings and I stood in awe as our newly discovered grandfather plucked grapefruits the size of softballs off a tremendous tree next to the driveway and put them into a small wooden crate.

Next, he filled a wrinkled grocery sack with huge oranges and handed it to me. My sister carried in ripe tomatoes using her shirt as a bowl. My brother, always up for mischief, disappeared behind the gate to explore the dangerous canal. We'd fish him out later when his cries for help echoed into the yard.

All these mysterious activities occurred while Grandpa remained mute yet smiling. His movements, slow and deliberate, belied his years. He appeared timeless and interchangeable with all his former relatives.

Step-Grandma was a horse of a different color. Her soft Georgian accent tickled our ears as she leapt excitedly from one topic of conversation to the next. Opal never seemed to take a breath.

Her rapid-fire questions about us and our future plans left no spaces for answers. She invited us to sit at a table laden with home-grown delicacies and freshly baked pies.

Iced tea and Pepsi orders were solicited as she bustled about to place more edibles on the overburdened table.

The only regret I felt on this momentous visit was a mourning for the years lost before fitting this huge missing piece into our family-tree puzzle.

My greatest family memories are of the decades of Thanksgiving dinners hosted at their home and the annual sharing of the same-day birthdays of my grandfather and me. Opal always made us a carrot cake without raisins, but with extra walnuts, from their neighbor's overhanging tree.

Unbeknownst before our meeting, I was delighted to learn this was my grandpa's favorite cake, too.

Uncle Allen, a good-hearted soul, lived his life always looking for the positive side of tragedy, and he endured many of them. From severe illnesses as a child to two crazy ex-wives and a socially debilitating near-deafness, he soldiered on in childlike innocence.

Grandpa's reticence didn't allow for intimacy, and try as I might, I never had a meaningful conversation with him. When questioned, he shyly smiled and hunched his shoulders up and down, indicating God knows what.

In these instances, Opal would come to his rescue and give her interpretation of what he might be thinking.

I held onto the hope that because we shared the same birthday, and he was only forty-four years older than me, we would develop a relationship akin to some of my friends' experiences with their grandparents. The closest we ever got occurred at his funeral.

My grief-stricken grandmother nodded silent approval to me as our circle of family recited The Lord's Prayer at his open coffin, and I reached in to take Grandpa's cold hand to complete the circle.

The result of my grandparents' loss of nearly everything in their flight from the dusty Midwest, and their struggle to start over from scratch, triggered a tendency not to waste anything. These days it's referred to as hoarding.

For many years, my parents overlooked Grandma's overabundance of kitchenware, clothing, knick-knacks, linens, and every other item as the result of them being "collectors."

My grandparents and uncle haunted flea markets and garage sales each weekend, “saving” money on everything that caught their eyes as possibly being valuable. They spoke of selling these bargains for a profit, but nothing ever left the house.

Following my uncle’s untimely death, Grandma enlisted my parents and I to assist her in disposing of his possessions. We came to understand the depth of their obsessions, and the same shock reverberated after Grandma’s death.

These three people, the kindest, gentlest members of my entire family tree, never touched a drop of alcohol.

There is no such thing as a perfect family, or even a perfect person, but they came close.

23

Harmless Drinkies

A not-so-subtle shift occurred as my father's military career ascended. The need to socialize was part and parcel of his advancement, and this instigated the necessity for providing alcohol at their required home dinner parties.

I remember my confusion at hearing the grownups' laughter escalate in tone and volume as they exchanged silly comments during dinner. My usually reticent father became the life of the party, and Mom busied herself refilling glasses with odd-colored liquids. My siblings and I were warned not to sip at the mysterious adult drinks.

One evening, as I passed a seating of six at the formal dining table near the entrance to our downstairs family room, my father called attention to his "lovely daughter who recently became a woman."

The reference to my private and embarrassing first period in front of strangers infused me with a hatred that took decades to cool.

Later, my mother attempted to console me with some drivel about him drinking too much alcohol, but my uninitiated psyche wasn't appeased, only disgusted.

My parents were a solid team, and my sister, my brother, and I always came in second. I believed us to be in a lopsided family but had nothing to compare it to.

Gradually, the smell of alcohol and my mother's cigarette smoke seemed normal.

I learned to keep a low profile when they entertained and swore to myself never to swallow a drop of the soul-altering drink.

I only recall one incident of my father's drinking causing my mother alarm.

One night after partying, Dad awaited the babysitter at the front door while Mom paid her from the bills in her purse. As I watched silently from my darkened bedroom doorway, my mom turned abruptly when Dad dropped the car keys to the floor and rubbed his face vigorously with both hands.

The look on the babysitter's face showed concern, tinged with fear, and my mother noticed.

Picking up the car keys, my mother instructed the high school girl to watch a little more television and promised to return in a short period of time. Mom ushered Dad out the door, and soon I heard one slam of a car door and the engine starting up.

Racing to my bedroom window, I witnessed my mother at the wheel and my father trotting unsteadily behind the car as they traversed to the end of the block. They disappeared around a corner and returned fifteen minutes later to the curb in front of the house.

My mother opened the front door, removed her hat, and called out to the puzzled teenager. Dad stood leaning against the doorframe, panting but steady.

Several years later, after the results of disappointing blood tests, Dad quit drinking alcohol cold turkey. Mother missed her five o'clock martini with my father but bravely kept up this tradition until her doctor cut her off in her seventies after two bouts of pancreatitis.

24

Hormones And Boys

As I looked forward to attending our brand-new high school, I couldn't predict the highlight of my one year there. I'd be half of a socially recognized couple with a cheerful young man who'd steal my heart.

Although I became a "new kid" once again as a freshman, I joined a crowd of 200 others in my class, making it almost a non-issue. My small junior high school class melded gradually with the other four Catholic school transferees.

How exciting and pleasurable it was to see scores of unfamiliar faces masking untold stories. The girls dreamed of dancing with gangly, handsome boys, and the boys went crazy thinking of all the new possibilities for romance.

One young man in my algebra class made my heart do funny things, but when he smiled at the pretty blonde with braces, my stomach hurt.

As my body nudged me towards womanhood, I developed an ache in my heart that prompted dreams of the type of loving relationship my parents attained. With little or no understanding of the trials they endured at my age, I blissfully imagined the acquisition of their level of commitment and solidarity to be relatively effortless.

After nine months of angst, euphoria, and desperation, my beloved and I went from strangers to people who blushed at five-word innocuous sentences as we passed in the hall. The only time he touched me was when we danced, and that was infrequently and in an auditorium full of students and chaperones.

We never shared a phone call or exchanged notes at school. Our innocent relationship existed only in our teenaged hearts.

When my dad received orders to report to the West Coast, the move was scheduled for the same night as my first boy/girl party at a friend's house.

I refused to leave before the event because my love had offhandedly passed me in the hall on the last day of the school term and said, "See you at the party!"

My mother intuited my feelings for the young man, and some heartstring of hers must have resurrected a similar experience with my father. She knew I would never see him again but couldn't bear to see me suffer the loss of one last opportunity to dance in his arms.

Dance we did. From the moment we met in the darkened basement festooned with streamers and balloons, we danced to each successive record. Not missing a step between the clicks of the forty-fives dropping onto the record player, we even slow danced to *The Twist* by Chubby Checker.

As the second dance had begun, he turned his face to mine as I nestled at his shoulder. When I looked up, he gave me my first kiss, swiftly and softly. He repeated the chaste kiss with every new song. I counted twenty-three, one every two and a half minutes, give or take.

Like Cinderella, I heard an announcement signal the end of my romantic evening and stopped dancing to memorize his face. The hostess of our party shouted above the music to tell me my parents were waiting in the car, and I was to hurry up and say goodbye.

As my love stared at me in shock, I hastened to tell him of my family's transfer to California, and I was ordered to depart that instant. I had no forwarding address or phone number to give him, only pain.

He froze, speechless, and watched me walk out of his life.

All the way to our new home I remained unreachable and distraught, wondering what I could have done to change our fate.

25

Beware Of Puma Eggs!

In the early 1960s, our next migration took us to the West Coast. Upon entering this wonderland, we gaped like the tourists we were at the sunny beaches, a boardwalk with countless amusements, and the sparkling ocean.

Suntanned teenagers in bikinis played volleyball and baked in the sun on colorful towels. Totally smitten, I vowed never to abandon this paradise.

As we settled into our home in sight of the Pacific Ocean, my previous doomed affair of the heart faded enough to notice a young man and his female companion pass by our front porch. Sitting on an old rocking chair afforded me privacy to mourn my lost life in the Midwest.

They paused, offered friendly hellos, and launched into a flurry of questions pertaining to our recent arrival. The conversation ended with an invitation to join them and their high school friends at the seashore the following day.

As they rounded the corner, I leapt from my perch and dashed into the kitchen, startling my mother, who only knew me to mope about the house as silently as a ghost since our arrival.

"Where is my bathing suit?" I shouted with excitement. "I'm meeting some kids at the beach near the river mouth tomorrow!"

Dropping her dish towel onto a hook, she sprinted after me as I climbed the wooden steps two at a time.

That summer, my slender figure added bumps and curves, and my old swimming suit looked incredible to me but indecent to my mother. She left my room and returned with her old swimming suit and insisted I wear it instead. *Ugh!*

My new friends returned the next morning, as promised, to find my Midwestern white skin glowing from beneath an oversized sweatshirt borrowed from my father. White socks and sneakers covered my tender feet, and my skinny legs weren't my best feature. To top off the look, my mother had slathered my nose with zinc oxide and stuck a baseball cap on my head.

Clad in flip flops and casual swim attire over tanned bodies, my new friends exchanged amused glances but invited me to join them on my first of many walks to the beach. Tim whispered a little too loudly to Trixie, "Geez, all she needs is a camera around her neck."

Venturing out obliviously into life as the new kid once again, I didn't realize my acquisition of the dreaded, additional moniker, "Tourist!"

Winded but able to keep up the pace for the two miles to the beach, I flopped into the sand near the mouth of the local river, known for its wandering ways. Sometimes it broke through a sand dam and joined the ocean, but when in a lazy mood, it stopped short and turned into a shallow lake for the little kids to play in.

Lying on my stomach, I tried to blend in with the fifteen or so assorted local teenagers, some on beach blankets, others sprawled on the hot sand. I noticed a spray-painted warning on the side of a steep cliff on the opposite side of the river.

It blazed: *Danger!! Beware of the puma eggs!!*

I leaned over to Trixie, interrupting her gossip with a girl whose makeup looked like she was going to a prom, and asked, "What are puma eggs?"

"Barnacles on the rocks." Trixie snorted. "It's a joke we play on tourists, like giving them fake directions when they're lost."

I dared not reprimand her for their un-Christian-like behavior so early in our friendship, and she returned to her gossip.

Not twenty minutes later, one of our gang, a very good-looking young guy named Larry, ran to our loose circle, threw himself into the sand, and began rolling about with laughter. Ears perked up, and questions flew.

When Larry managed to collect himself, the story unfolded:

"I was passing the lifeguard station when I heard this tourist lady shouting up at the lifeguard. She had her kid by the arm and was pointing to his bloody legs. She wanted to know what to put on the puma egg bites her son got while climbing on the rocks near the cliff."

My heart went out to them, but I forced a laugh anyway as the rest of the crowd howled at the stupid tourists.

With sunburned face, legs, and feet, I trudged home behind my energetic new friends, barely making it up the steps to our front door. As I reached for the knob, my mother yanked the door open, pushed my brother and I nose to nose, and shrieked, "Look at Junior's legs! He's covered in puma egg bites! The lifeguard wouldn't even help us!"

I felt my fledgling social life shrivel and die.

26

Social Divide

The small town, dissected by the diverse societies of two high schools, proved difficult for me to navigate. An unspoken line separated the heathen locals from the Catholic kids.

Fate laughed as I spent my first wonderful summer forging friendships with the so-called delinquents.

"Those kids" smoked, drank, and experienced pregnancies out of wedlock, I was warned. Repeatedly cautioned to keep my distance from them, as if their evil habits might be contagious, I felt torn.

Not all the locals were heathens, but the nuns and many of my friends' parents, including my own, endorsed the theory.

I now understand how my parents knew these things. They grew up smack in the middle of the "bad kids," but now I felt my world constricting to one less entertaining and adventuresome. I was sure Grandma Rachael would agree with me.

As the school year commenced, I found myself suddenly ridiculed by my former peer group as a Catholic high school loser. With no common social denominator to link us, the friendships ceased.

Outcast, I turned to my new social arena as the “new kid” yet again.

At least I showed up with a tan.

27

Important Years

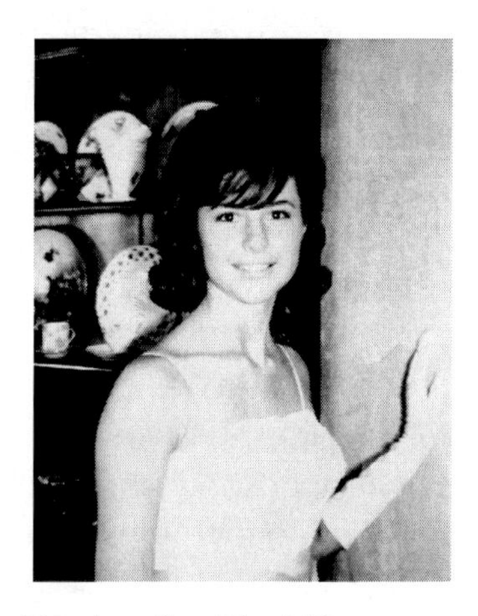

Posing for First Prom

Although the local public high school boasted over a thousand students, my Catholic counterpart barely served two hundred. The sophomore class consisted of forty-two students, most of whom had forged friendships during grade-school days.

My Midwestern accent trumpeted my tourist status as I was forced to introduce myself to the class. With all eyes upon me, the Sister pointed to the last seat near the exit door, and I scurried there, praying for invisibility.

With only five classrooms to traverse, going from one subject's destination to another didn't require much decision making. I observed that the lemmings in the hall moved counterclockwise, and if one of them missed the exit to a proper classroom, the journey continued along the short loop until the exit reappeared.

Recently transferring from my huge new high school of one thousand students in our freshman class, with multiple floors of classrooms, I felt ridiculous in this ancient building, yet grateful for the ease of the system.

At the completion of my first day, a pretty girl from my homeroom sidled up to me and introduced herself with a cheerful, "Hi there! You're new! I'm Sherry. I was a new kid when I came here in fifth grade," she continued. "Stick with me, and I'll show you the ropes." She added a conspiratorial smile that highlighted her singular dimple.

Many of the boys enjoyed a fresh face in the tight-knit school, and Sherry pointed out those flirting with me. With only one innocent relationship under my belt, I perceived her assistance and experience necessary to interpret the mysterious signals.

One tall, nice-looking boy in a letterman's sweater passed us in the hall at lunch time, barely raised his head in a subtle nod as he looked our way, and muttered, "Hey."

He kept moving down the hall.

"Ooooo, he likes you!" cooed my translator. "Seniors don't talk to sophomores. His name is Joe, and he's on the varsity basketball team. His shirt number is twenty-one."

I scoffed at her raised eyebrows and dismissed the incident.

When cheerleading tryouts were announced, Sherry insisted I join her for the event. The odds were with us since very few young ladies showed up to audition.

"New Kid" vanished as a junior varsity cheerleader emerged from her cocoon. I enjoyed the feeling of being a big fish in a little pond after years of feeling a ghost, coming and going with little or no fanfare.

The loquacious fellow, Joe, would prove to be my only legitimate high school boyfriend; someone I grew to love and trust.

We attended two proms together, and my mother enjoyed picking out my dresses and hairstyles as much as, or more than, I did. Dad dusted off the trusty camera and snapped us from every direction in our formal finest as we attempted to flee to the dance.

Stepping into a prom like a princess on Joe's arm, and slow dancing with him all night in the dim, decorated auditorium, produced some of my most treasured memories.

Guarded by a strict upbringing and an ever-present church influence, Joe's and my innocence remained intact during the relationship, yet these factors left us vulnerable to the temptations of the real world in later years.

Joe's similarity to my father both attracted and alarmed me. I sensed the distinct possibility of a relationship akin to my parents' with him, but my genes from Grandma Rachael demanded I find a path to independence first and foremost.

After a teenage love/hate turmoil of several years, Joe and I parted ways when he transferred to an out-of-state college. My three years at Holy Moley High (aka Sacred Heart High School) tested my confidence and self-esteem and introduced me to teenage angst. It felt like a lifetime of experiences crammed into an interminable, yet fleeting, eight hundred days.

My sister, Lynn, gregarious and sweet-tempered, garnered friendships with ease. Her grades proved mediocre, but she was content and popular.

As a young teen, Junior's model airplane hobby introduced him to sniffing glue. When this habit was thwarted by my all-knowing parents, he gradually moved into beer, and then hard alcohol in his high school years. The hellish nightmare of alcoholism had stealthily traversed the gene path from my parents' past to their only son.

For me, football games, prom, becoming editor of the school newspaper and a basketball princess, four years of Latin, and surviving the death of John F. Kennedy made for a promising basis for my future life at college. Dreams of writing for a major newspaper danced in my head.

However, after terrific stats on the SATs in English and math, my school advisor, Sister Mary Howard, joyfully revealed to my mother my life's calling indubitably was to be a really good "wife and mother."

At least I wasn't being recruited to her Order of Sisters, but I felt disappointed, nonetheless.

Little did I know Sister's prediction was uncanny, for I became a wife *three* times, and bore three children. Probably not what Sister envisioned.

28

Unfair Competition

Like my grandmothers and mother, I seemed to attract an inordinate amount of male attention. I chalked the dubious honor up to our cheerful dispositions and easygoing personalities. To be fair, I must also give credit to favorable genetic female attributes.

We ladies appreciated the positive differences in the sexes, and the fellas enjoyed our tendency to harmlessly flirt and the ability to belly laugh at their jokes.

The only drawback occurred when I brought boys home to meet the family. Invariably, they were drawn to my attractive mom, now only in her early thirties. Her youthful charm and fine looks, not to mention a great figure, caused friction between the two of us.

In addition to my perceived tug-of-war for my father's love and attention, now my male friends were added to the battle. Mom proved famous for lending a sympathetic ear when the young men suffered from relationship woes, and her advice was eagerly sought.

It seemed traitorous when she gave advice to my boyfriends concerning their dealings with me!

Too often I would return from school to find one or more of my former boyfriends huddled in the kitchen, sipping on the pink grapefruit juice she provided. Coke was too expensive, she said.

Raised in this environment, my mother naturally voiced approval when I rejected three marriage proposals before I entered college. "Chip off the old block" and all that.

29

Premature Decision

Four years on the West coast flew by, and Dad received word of his final transfer, indicating a return to the Midwest.

After enjoying the freedom of my first year in a Bay Area all-girls Catholic college, I balked at my parents' demand for me to leave paradise and rejoin the family in the depressing Midwest.

I begged to remain in the sheltered college, but they felt uneasy leaving me unchaperoned at holiday periods. I argued that I was eighteen years old, an adult, but having married in their young teens, they feared the temptations I might face.

Their only exception to leaving with them was for me to marry, and thus transfer the responsibility of myself to a husband. A woman's independence, at least in my parents' eyes, was not an option. I felt trapped in the Victorian era, not the mid-1960s.

Dating was part of my regimen, but I felt too young to settle down.

Fate offered me the chance to marry a handsome twenty-year-old apprentice plumber who wanted the freedom to move out of his parents' house. Our short-term goals matched, but having experienced lives pre-arranged since childhood, we didn't harbor any defined long-term goals to consolidate.

The first time I met Mike's parents, Bub and Marie, I fell in love with his dad.

His mom was intelligent, strong, and considered Mike the favorite of their five children. The first child, a girl, had died shortly after birth.

Bub seemed the calmest, most easy-going person I ever met, and I fantasized about a life with him as my dad, instead of the one I had been given.

Mike's parents didn't give much thought to Mike and me dating, and I always enjoyed the homey welcome I received in their simple, unstructured world.

My mother's advice for a successful marriage consisted of four words, "Marry your best friend."

Dad stayed out of it.

So, after dating for three months and developing a good friendship and vague romantic feelings for one another, Mike and I decided to get married in the distant future.

To our dismay, upon sharing the news with my parents, my father insisted on a short engagement while muttering something about "avoiding trouble."

We were both sexually innocent and didn't understand the implication.

Dad demanded a wedding by the end of summer. A date for August 31 was deemed acceptable by my mother, and she sprang into action. A church to be reserved, gowns picked out, flowers, and a reception filled her thoughts. More excited than I, she left me in the dust.

My new fiancé and I looked at each other and wondered what the hell we'd gotten ourselves into. It appeared too late to amend our decision or cancel it altogether if we changed our minds in a few months. I was barely nineteen, and Mike had recently turned twenty. We had nowhere near the skills our parents did when they entered their married lives but told ourselves we'd vow to try our best.

Five months later, against our wishes for a simple ceremony, the supersized wedding my mother dreamed of for herself long ago was celebrated in style.

As my father and I awaited the signal to approach the altar, both decked out in wedding splendor, I looked him in the eyes and confessed, "I'm making a big mistake, Dad."

Obviously shaken and influenced by my mother's shame at a non-wedding at this point, he forced a smile and quipped, "Just pre-wedding jitters, honey. It's showtime!"

The irony of our premature wedding is that my father's transfer to the Midwest was delayed, shortly after our ceremony, for a full year. With that change of circumstance, in all probability, Mike and I wouldn't have married, and our children would never have been born.

PART III

HEAVEN & HELL ON EARTH

30

From Two To Three

After the wedding reception, Mike and I drove to Carmel for the official start of our honeymoon, with the plan of driving to Disneyland the following day.

As we unpacked the Volkswagen, I searched frantically for my small overnight bag. Since my birth control pills resided there, along with my beauty products, its disappearance caused great alarm. Neither of us remembered loading the article, so this necessitated an hour-long drive back to my former home.

My sister, Lynn, met us at the door and immediately burst into champagne-induced tears. "Did you break up already?" she wailed.

Shushing her the best I could and noticing my missing case by the closet door, I snagged the bag and told her not to worry.

We lit out of town and drove the hour back to our hotel. I felt glad for the reprieve and its putting distance between the time when our relationship as friends would transform mysteriously into becoming lovers.

Upon our attempted check-in, the seasoned clerk questioned our baby faces, then demanded identification and a copy of our marriage license. He snickered as he handed us our key.

The wedding night proved interesting in a clinical sort of way, with no reaction from my husband as I noted the blood on our sheets the following morning. He only inquired if I had cut myself shaving. I rethought the value of saving my precious virginity for him and felt cheated somehow.

After a short honeymoon trip surrounded by children at the theme park, and a harrowing thirty-minute trek in and out of Tijuana for gas, my new husband and I attempted to adjust to a new life as grownups. The learning curve was gradual, at best.

After five months of settling into a routine, I shared some unbelievable news with Mike. We would become parents a month after our first wedding anniversary.

Planning for a family wasn't akin to a life as an independent couple, with time for movies and card games with friends after working hours.

Our first small apartment seemed wonderful until the noise from neighbors, mostly students and young singles, drove us to a fourplex with a second bedroom for the baby.

I had been working at an insurance company as a secretary when we married and continued to do so until my seventh month of pregnancy. Mike worked forty hours a week as a plumber and went to trade school several nights a week to become a journeyman.

We decided I would quit my job and stay home after our baby was born, despite the expected monetary challenges.

Collecting inexpensive baby items and searching for an affordable crib was exciting. A few girlfriends with new babies lent me used maternity outfits and outgrown baby clothes. I made colorful curtains for the nursery with an old sewing machine my mom gave me.

My life seemed full and perfect.

Early in the pregnancy, I tripped and fell while crossing a street on our evening walk. Mike blamed himself for not catching me before I hit the pavement. We worried about possible damage to our developing baby.

Several days later, I started spotting and sought advice from my obstetrician. After his examination, he cautioned that I might lose the baby. He told me he didn't think it was a result of the fall but that something might be wrong with the fetus, and this was nature's way of furthering "survival of the fittest."

I was horrified! I counted on this baby to bring me purpose, to be a person who would depend on me and love me unconditionally. My marriage of convenience was impersonal, more friendship than love. With my family still living far away, I felt so lonely. I begged the doctor to save my precious child.

Against his better judgment, he gave me a hormone shot and warned it might not stop a miscarriage. He reiterated I might be bringing a damaged baby into my life. Innocently, I replied I'd deal with it.

I tried my best to trust God and prayed fervently. In addition to weekly Mass, I attended nine weeks of Novena services for the intention of our baby's well-being. The spotting stopped, and the baby continued to develop.

I was still of petite stature and underweight at twenty, From the side, however, my stomach looked like a basketball. The baby kicked and stretched, and I knew he or she would love me as a mom.

Nearing the third trimester of my pregnancy, I dreamt that I was able to see into my uterus and view the kicking baby. To my surprise and dismay, it was not a baby inside me at all but a small alligator, complete with toothsome jaws and jagged tail. It swished and twirled as if in pain. I knew, somehow, I wasn't carrying a normal baby, and this rocked my spiritual and emotional worlds.

In the morning, I prayed for the dream to fade, but it resolutely remained firmly in my mind. Each time the baby kicked, I put my hand on my moving skin and imagined terrible things.

I had finished my nine weeks of Novenas and started a second series, this time pleading with God to let my baby be born alive so I could baptize it before it died. I believed in my heart and soul that I would need this favor to ensure my being able to spend eternity with a child I most likely wouldn't know on Earth.

Explaining my sudden lack of enthusiasm for the coming birth was difficult. Relating the dream to my mom and husband only produced disbelief and chiding.

When my girlfriends gave me a baby shower, I struggled to show excitement and pleasure as I unwrapped the many gifts of tiny socks and beautiful blankets.

In my soul, I fought the darkness and prayed that I was mistaken but couldn't seem to shake the vision.

31

Birth Day

On the afternoon before the baby was due, I stood on the back porch tending my potted geraniums when water suddenly flowed between my legs and flooded onto the landing. Shocked, I didn't know what to do first. *Should I find a towel? Call my husband at work? Would he be out on a project?*

Dear God, I prayed, *help me!*

When Mike finally arrived, I held a towel between my legs as he hustled to find my prepared hospital suitcase. He called my mom and told her to meet us at the hospital. She had flown in from the Midwest on the day before, was staying with a long-time friend, and planned to stay a week after the birth to assist with her first grandchild.

The admittance process was lengthy, but eventually I found myself tucked into a labor room with my mother at my side. Mike was delegated to a waiting room as was the custom in the mid-1960s.

As my contractions increased in intensity, I begged God to protect me and my child with every painful breath.

The hospital's call to my obstetrician reached him at a dinner party having cocktails. My mother appeared uneasy when she overheard this bit of information because my parents knew him well, and of his propensity to be more than a social drinker.

In that darkened labor room, with my mom coming in and out between nurse visits, I hugged my baby and hoped the intense pain I was experiencing would be over soon. After seven hours of labor, and no visit from my doctor, my mother was furious. It was after ten o'clock in the evening.

Nearing eleven o'clock, my mother summoned the nurse for pain medication when I cried out in unbelievable agony. The nurse peered between my bent knees and alarmed my mother with, "Oh, she's crowning!"

As the nurse darted from the room, I turned to my mother with wide eyes. This was my first baby, and I really had no idea what that meant.

I was told to put my knees together as they hurriedly rolled my bed into a brightly lit room. My mother and husband remained in the hall. I looked up to see my doctor putting on a clean gown. A nurse behind me whispered, "I hope we got enough coffee in him."

My familiar doctor, now masked, turned and faced the gurney. He asked the nurse to prepare a spinal block. The nurse reminded him that the baby was crowning, but he told her I needed pain relief now. I watched her face register disapproval as he accepted the incredibly long needle and syringe.

"Roll her on her side and tuck her knees up. Hold her so she doesn't move," he instructed.

With contractions wracking my body and the baby so close to presenting, the nurses did their best to keep me still.

I felt a jab in my spine and cried out.

The doctor cursed and indicated that he did not find the right spot. He ordered another injection to be prepared.

I pleaded and cried for the pain to cease. *What is this delay doing to my baby?*

My doctor, still unsteady from a night of drinking, raised his voice, "Keep her still this time."

Another painful jab, and then soon, miraculously, the pain eased and ceased. As the nurse rolled me to my back, I noticed that I had no feeling in my legs.

The doctor sat on a small stool and looked up at me through my legs. In a short period of time, he pronounced matter of factly, "It's a girl."

I heard a pitiful squeaking sound.

My mind flashed back to prenatal pamphlets indicating the signs of a healthy baby at birth. The first: a lusty cry; the second: tight, shaking fists; the third: a pot-bellied appearance.

I strained to see between my gowned knees to peek at my beloved baby. The doctor unceremoniously slapped her on my stomach, and I gazed in wonder at her beautiful face, plentiful dark hair, and chubby legs. There was a squeaking sound instead of a lusty cry.

Mentally, I added the kitten-like mew to the sight of her fully opened left hand reaching slowly toward her face. On observing her flat tummy and bulging chest, maternal panic set in, and I reached out to her.

"Don't let her touch the baby," barked my physician as he cut the cord. A nurse whisked my "happily ever after" dreams off my deflated belly and lay her in a prepared baby container on my right.

My eyes attempted to memorize her features as my heart telepathically sent her all my love.

When the doctor issued orders, the nurses scrambled. My entire universe existed in that tiny unreachable cubicle so cruelly nearby, and my tears erupted when they rolled my baby out of the room.

The doctor finished stitching me up, rose from his stool, and gave my hand a squeeze as he struggled to explain that there were complications. I'd be informed of her condition as soon as they could determine the extent of the problems.

When my mother joined me, I made her promise to find a priest as soon as possible to baptize my child. Thankfully, one was procured, and the redemptive sacrament was administered as she lay in intensive care.

My despondency at descending into this hell lessened as my assurance for her admission into a loving heaven solidified.

I never got to hold her, to tell her how much I wanted and loved her. I never saw her again.

My faith in God was beyond shaken.

32

Tidal Wave From Hell

Early the next morning, I sat up abruptly, nauseated, as I searched for a bedpan. My spinal medication had worn off, and my stomach rejected all its contents. I was disoriented and had forgotten the stern warning of the nurse not to sit up for an extended number of hours or else face a lingering migraine headache.

Now my head and eyes experienced an overwhelming aching, and pain filled the few remaining places in my body unscathed so far. The horror of the previous evening consumed my mind and soul.

I had been awakened at some dark hour when a masked surgeon attempted to explain my six-pound, six-ounce, nineteen-inch daughter's difficulties.

Following as best as I could, I watched as he used his hands against his chest to indicate his sternum. She had a birth defect that did not close a hole between the area of her heart and intestines. Since she was carried head down, her intestines leaked into her chest cavity. This explained her flat tummy and expanded chest area.

The surgeon wanted to operate to close the hole and reposition the intestines. Once that part of the surgery was finished, supposedly her heart would move over to the center of her chest and her lungs could then inflate properly.

He had documents for me to sign to allow the surgery and handed me a pen.

Confused and alone, I begged him with my weeping eyes.

"Time is of the essence," he replied. "She won't survive without the surgery, and even though we can't guarantee she'll make it, at least there's a chance."

I took the pen with trembling fingers and signed my name without having a chance to discuss the life-altering decision with my husband or mother.

Wracked in pain and grief, I waited in my bed for word from the doctors. The migraine thwarted my attempt at sleep, and the nurse's medication offered no relief.

Hours later, before dawn, the surgeon returned, blood speckling his smock. He launched into an explanation of his labors.

"We opened her chest cavity at the sternum to below her navel…"

He paused as I gaped in disbelief at the vision my mind displayed.

"Did you give her anesthetic first?" I raised my voice. I needed confirmation that she did not feel any agony or terror.

To this day, I cannot believe the cruelty of his reply. "No," he said. "She was too small for..."

I didn't comprehend anything after the word "No."

He transformed into a merciless demon before my eyes as he continued with some strange sense of pride, "We were able to bring the intestines into the proper cavity and close the hole. We moved her heart over where it was supposed to be, and her lungs inflated."

This seemed like good news, and I hung on his every word.

"Unfortunately," he continued in a softer voice, "when she still wasn't responding, we discovered the valves in her heart were reversed. We don't have the ability to perform this type of heart surgery on infants currently. We aren't sure how much brain damage may have resulted after her heart stopped a couple of times. Our recommendation is that you take her off oxygen and let her go."

"I'm sorry," he managed. He then added, "The nurse will bring you paperwork to authorize this. You may want to do this as soon as possible; she is probably in a lot of pain."

I prayed to die with her as I signed my name to that wretched legal document. I truly felt as if I were killing her. Experiencing the incredible physical and mental anguish, my soul went dark.

Blessedly, overcome by additional medication, I mercifully and dreamlessly slept for a few hours.

I was awakened by a harsh hand and frantic voice.

My poor husband, aware of "complications" when he left the hospital in the early morning hours, had returned after a few hours' sleep with a bouquet of flowers for me and to check in on the baby.

Mike had visited his baby daughter's private room before going home, so he returned there unawares. She lay in the small enclosed container, still and blue. It took him a few moments to realize that she was dead. Panicked beyond belief, Mike rushed to the nurses' station.

They appeared alarmed, but not surprised, to learn from him that the baby had passed and regretted his witnessing such a distressing scene.

Our poor little angel had died alone and in pain. It was unconscionable, unbelievably cruel. The vision of her in that condition haunted him for the rest of his life.

As Mike stood over me in such terrible shape shouting, "What happened?", all I could do was to open my arms and cry with him. He climbed into the hospital bed next to me, and we shared our last unguarded moment.

From then forward, our hearts were hardened by the shared tragedy. We individually swore that nothing could ever hurt us that much again.

We named her Kathleen.

Upon release from the hospital, the consensus of both families was that I not be left alone. My episiotomy stitches proved infected and caused me waves of lower abdominal agony. I lay on my side on a couch in Bub and Marie's living room, praying for relief from the inadequate pain pills.

Bub volunteered to take the first shift and cared for me tenderly.

He couldn't help but recall the tragedy of his and Marie's daughter's death. This opportunity to stand watch, and the need to ease my pain, generated from his previously broken heart.

Curled in a fetal position on the small couch, I watched the glow from Bub's fake fireplace and attempted not to think or feel. The rhythmic sound of his rocking chair as he read his fishing magazine lulled me into a blessed, dreamless sleep.

His kindness towards me during that wretched time will never be forgotten.

33

First Christmas

The tragedy was overwhelming, and my only support was a distraught husband. We each blamed ourselves for a tragedy that was no one's fault.

I was so angry with God. *How could He take an innocent baby and subject her to such a cruel, short life?* God and I had always been close. *What had I done to deserve such a tragedy?*

God was holding all the cards. My baptized daughter was in heaven with Him, and if I didn't play by His rules, I would never see her again. My first taste of an eternal hell was bitter and invited despair. Although I continued to attend Mass every week, I cast down my eyes and grumbled instead of praying. Feelings of loss mingled with repressed hate, and I had no one to share my confusion with.

My father, who had suffered unimaginable trauma in the war, found our situation so distressing he was tearfully mute in my presence. My mother had entered my home while I was still hospitalized and removed Kathleen's pink and blue bassinet, her crib filled with stuffed animals, and all her tiny baby clothes.

When I returned home, I found the baby's room empty and her belongings in a large cedar chest, resembling a coffin, in the closet.

My parents' shared life-long survival response kicked in. I was told it would be best for me to forget the whole episode and look forward to having another pregnancy. Not having suffered a loss like this themselves, they couldn't differentiate between their life experiences and mine.

The baby's burial and short funeral service happened while I was still in the hospital. My mother insisted that I not be given the location of the grave to keep me from "haunting" it, and thus not move forward emotionally.

It was not until three months later, on Christmas Eve, that I discovered where my child's cemetery plot was located. My husband and I were both still in deep mourning as I challenged him that night.

Looking at our half-heartedly decorated Christmas tree, I calmly said that I would kill myself if he did not disclose where the baby was buried; that I couldn't be away from Kathleen on Christmas Eve.

"But I promised!" Mike said too loudly.

"Then I'll kill myself," I responded calmly.

Mike went to find his car keys and we drove to the cemetery in silence as the sun began to set. I struggled to remember the route through tear-filled eyes. My husband gently took my hand,

and we reverently walked over an expanse of graves in the "baby cemetery."

One stone marker after another proclaimed misery and loss with names and dates and faded flowers. It felt more like Halloween than Christmas.

Abruptly, Mike stopped and looked down at a small square stone with the numbers "957" engraved into it. The permanent memorial marker with Kathleen's name and year of birth hadn't arrived yet.

I looked down at the pathetically small rectangle of dirt under which Kathleen's tiny body lay and imagined her dark hair and lovely small face. I wanted to lay on top of this space and quit breathing forever so that I could hold her tight and warm her.

My husband had not wanted to discuss our loss, but now his slumping shoulders heaved up and down as he sobbed and slowly dropped to his knees.

"Merry Christmas, Kathleen," I managed to whisper before joining him on the damp earth, surrounded by scores of other infants' graves.

34

One Day At A Time

Mike became increasingly depressed. Not only did we have a mortgage and other normal bills, but now we had enormous hospital and burial expenses to pay.

I became obsessed with longing for another baby, but my husband was reluctant to chance another disappointment.

Seventeen months after our daughter died, we were blessed with a healthy son, but each of us held back some part of our hearts out of fear of another loss.

I felt broken and didn't know how to fix myself. Mike grew steadily more distant. These were the days before therapy and support groups. People just suffered in silence and coped badly.

As our finances improved, we purchased a modest new home and I unexpectedly became pregnant again. Our son, Chris, was fourteen months old, and our fragile marriage was hanging by a thread. This would be my third baby in four years, and I was not physically or emotionally up to it. The next seven months were difficult.

The new baby, a perfect little girl, we named Lauren. From the moment of birth, she was a charmer, and we all rejoiced. Blonde and blue eyed, she did not resemble her angel sister, so there was no feeling of her replacing a lost sibling. She was her own person.

My life was filled with two active children in diapers. It seemed that as one slept, the other was awake. With a house, yard, and dog added to my daily chores, I was approaching burnout.

One night as I was finally drifting off to sleep, I heard one of the children call, "Mommy!"

I concentrated more intently, trying to decide which one it was, but when the call repeated, I wasn't sure if it was my son or daughter.

Reluctantly, I pulled back the covers and crept silently to our open bedroom door. I listened from the hall for a sound from the children's separate bedrooms, one to my left and the other on the right.

It was silent. I tiptoed to my daughter's room and observed her fast asleep on her side facing me, her favorite blanket snuggled to her chin.

That's funny, I thought. *It sounded like her voice.*

I stepped softly to my son's door and noted he was soundly sleeping on his back.

As I turned to go back to bed, I had an overwhelming feeling of a presence in the hall. Without thinking, I scolded, "Don't ever do that again, Kathleen! You scared Mommy."

Switching out the hall light, I hurried back to bed, my heart racing.

I have forever regretted those words, for I never heard my baby calling me again.

35

Spirit Visit

One afternoon, as my mother drove five-month old Lauren and me to a doctor's appointment, we stopped at a red light and waited. The baby was hunched in her car seat, trying to fit a small teddy bear into her mouth. Mom and I laughed at her expression as her tongue licked the fuzzy head.

Suddenly, Lauren dropped the bear and stared above the dashboard in fascination. Noticing her attention perk up, as if she heard a strange noise, Mom and I turned in unison and locked eyes over Lauren's head, then we curiously observed the dashboard. Nothing seemed to be there.

Lauren clapped her tiny hands, giggled in the cute way small babies do, and tried to baby talk to whomever she was obviously observing. She leaned backward into the car seat and pushed invisible fingers from her tummy as her giggling became laughter.

As we continued to stare, Mom whispered, "Lauren sees an angel!"

"No, it's her sister!" I gasped as I felt the same otherworldly presence from the recent hallway incident.

As I spoke, Lauren stopped giggling, leaned for her bear, and forgot the dashboard, as well as whatever interaction formerly occurred there. Kathleen had vanished.

Even though I never heard from her again, we knew that Kathleen remembered and loved us, as we did her.

36

Crossing The Line

After Lauren's birth, I consulted with my obstetrician concerning new methods of birth control. The Church's teachings forbid anything other than the rhythm method, but my brother was living proof of its unreliability.

Old family stories of seven living children per household gave me nightmares.

My doctor informed me of a new gadget referred to as "the coil." As I recall, the implant of this device into the cervix caused an irritation designed to discharge an embryo. The coil would come to be known as an IUD.

"It's only a small mass of cells, not a real baby," my doctor insisted.

Grasping at theoretical straws, I attempted to thwart moral warnings rising within me from my soul. However, thoughts of another pregnancy tortured me with worse visions.

The device implanted, I consented to the sexual advances of my young husband and prayed.

After a delayed monthly cycle, I doubled over with pain more severe than the usual cramps. I bled excessively, but not enough to warrant a trip to the doctor.

I reluctantly accepted that the coil had performed its duty, and succumbing to deep remorse, insisted my husband have a vasectomy.

37

Great Divide

Now my husband preferred drinking large quantities of cheap beer with former high school buddies to coming home after work, and we continued to grow apart. Their group involvement with marijuana, an illegal substance whose use could incur jail time, terrified me.

Mike's depression worsened, and he found little emotional energy for his children or me. I suggested a physical exam with our doctor, hoping some miracle medication might help him return to the fun-loving partner of my past.

Bub and Marie offered little insight into Mike's decline other than to remark that as a child, he was moody and sensitive.

After ten years of living in a deteriorating marriage, I suffered from an ulcer, and my husband wouldn't go to counseling with me.

"It's your problem," he insisted. "You go."

I went to an attorney instead.

My four-year-old daughter had noticed my silent tears after her father left the dinner table in anger the previous night. Lauren had whispered, "What did I do now to make you cry, Mommy?"

Being divorced was not better than being in a bad marriage, only different.

I recalled the courage of my grandmother, Rachael, who survived this same situation, and I bravely determined to make it work for my own decimated family.

After the home was sold, and the meager profits divided, my two young children and I rented an apartment.

I made a game of our reduced circumstances when possible. Every Sunday after Mass, I rewarded us with a long walk to our amusement park where we blew $5.00 on one game, or ride, each week.

After enjoying our treat, we walked the long distance home, cheerfully planning for next Sunday's choice of entertainment.

One Sunday at Mass, an ancient missionary nun came to beg for money to fund a Catholic children's home in a war-torn country. She brought the congregation to tears with vivid descriptions of the young people's plight.

The saintly woman promised that God would bless us four-fold if we generously donated. As she shuffled back to her seat, my children and I turned to one another and silently nodded assent.

As the offering basket passed to us, I placed our $5.00 treat money atop many other donations. After communion, when my eyes were closed, praying for my own little family, my daughter tugged on my sleeve. The children knew better than to interrupt Mommy's time with God, and I didn't respond. Lauren persisted.

I turned to give her a negative look but was shocked to see her holding up a $20 bill. Her eyes were round and her mouth agape.

"Where did you get that?" I whispered. I feared she had taken it out of the contribution basket.

"Something made me look in your wallet, and I found it there," she whispered loudly, as children do. Chris turned and took in the miracle. "It's four times as much, just like the Sister said."

Thanks to a generous God, we had money for four trips to the boardwalk, and my children learned a positive experience about being charitable. I explained, of course, that the return is not always monetary, but being good does beget more good.

38

The Real World

As a single woman, I was deemed a threat to my married friends. Unpartnered for the first time in many years, I hungered for adult company.

My ex-husband had taken up with a much younger woman, and she decided he couldn't support her and an ex-wife at the same time.

Mike saw his children only rarely, much to their distress. Now he had the nerve to come to me saying he would disappear altogether unless I gave up my paltry alimony.

I bargained an exchange for some cheap disputed personal property, and my little family took a major hit in our budget. We survived, but meals got leaner.

My parents were sympathetic to our plight, but my mother subscribed to, "You made your bed, now sleep in it." Having endured extreme hardship in her own life, she expected me to rise to the occasion unassisted.

My silent dad recalled his difficult life with a single mother and a small sister and prayed for us but offered little encouragement to me or his grandchildren.

I floundered but eventually found Tammy, a high school girlfriend, in the same circumstances.

She was blonde and blue-eyed, with enviable legs that she showcased with short skirts. She claimed her ex-husband's alcoholism caused their marriage's demise, although her own tolerance for drink was legendary.

We clung to each other as if shipwrecked on the same desert island, comparing our stories. Each sharing of our concerns and ideas for reconstructing our lives gave us hope and engendered courage.

Both of us feared for our children and their fathers' seeming abandonment of them. Alimony and child support checks appeared unpredictably or sometimes not at all.

Tammy and I foresaw our freedom as unemployed wives evolving into the slavery of working single mothers. But, for now, we took advantage of the few free months we would eke out until our lives crashed.

We took turns cooking and enjoyed card games at each other's homes while our similarly aged children played, oblivious to their tenuous circumstances and disoriented mothers. Chardonnay completed the threesome of our social grouping. We spent more money on wine than food.

Tammy's alcoholic parents offered her no assistance, and her father placed all blame for her failed marriage squarely in her camp. Tammy's mother, dominated by her rage-prone husband, secretly supported her daughter's escape from a husband like her father.

Unable to simply watch from the sidelines, my mother set me up on a blind date with the owner of a sandwich shop my parents frequented. The man was pleasant, she told me, and divorced with a teenage son. This man, several years older than me, might be a good catch, she added with a wink.

To thwart her further husband-trolling for me, I accepted a date when he called.

Paul appeared to be a decade older than me, and little remained of the hair on his head. He told me he was lonely, that he found me attractive, and brought us food. Fresh deli sandwiches, potato chips, and ice cream from his shop were his blessed tokens of affection.

As Paul observed my preference of wine over soft drinks, he began to include a couple of fine bottles of wine with each visit and graciously uncorked and poured my many glasses per evening.

This gentlemanly gesture was rewarded occasionally after the children were asleep even though I never developed an emotional tie to the kind man.

Alcohol was not my friend but stood by me through thick and thin, nonetheless.

Chris and Lauren loved being indulged and enjoyed Paul's company. We continued dating until his jealous teenage son started making threats against my children, then we broke up.

My new life was complicated.

Tammy called one afternoon to tell me of a new dance spot in town. Her brother and his wife recently treated her to drinks and appetizers there. When the D.J. turned on the overhead disco ball, and the speakers to full blast, the dance floor filled with revelers.

Single men lined the bar, looking for dance partners. Several of the men asked her to dance and for her phone number. She was so excited that I barely kept up with her descriptions of this new-age heaven.

Tammy refused to give out her number but had promised a man to meet with him the coming Tuesday night. He would bring a friend and asked her to do the same.

Tammy pleaded mercilessly, told me we could share a sitter, and wrung a promise from me to accompany her to the dance club.

Equally excited and dubious, I poured over my meager mommy wardrobe, looking for something resembling a thirty-year-old's dancing outfit.

The promised young men clicked their beer bottles as Tammy led me to their table. Without any experience of meeting strangers in a bar, my antenna went up but couldn't focus a clear signal.

After they bought us a couple of glasses of wine, and danced us into breathlessness, I forgot about the need for skepticism.

Tammy's date was a hefty sheriff's deputy named Luke and his friend, Marty, was recently released from the Army. These seemed like good credentials.

Long story short, each of us couples dated for a short while, and with all the wine and our thirst for attention and affection, Tammy and I succumbed to their baser instincts.

Feeling my dignity and moral standards slipping away, I broke off my relationship with Marty and encouraged Tammy to do the same. Her mother's role model of passivity caused her to falter.

Her boyfriend, Luke, realized my bad influence and showed up drunk at my door one evening. My children slept in a nearby room, so I innocently let him into my apartment to halt his incessant knocking.

The hulking deputy sat forlornly on the corner of my couch, uninvited, and proceeded to tell me his heart was breaking. Confused, I sat at the other end and asked if he wanted some hot tea since I now smelled the alcohol on his breath.

Abruptly, Luke lunged and pushed me down on the couch, pulling at my jeans. "You'd better stay quiet unless you want your children to see this," he warned.

He growled in my ear that I needed a lesson as I fought him pulling off my underwear. My arms pinned behind me, I pleaded in vain for him to stop. His eyes burned like a demon's, and his hot, boozy breath reeked of hell.

His jeans were at his knees when I shut my eyes and felt him struggle to push himself inside me. I cried out in terror and disbelief. When he finished with me, he stood to pull up his pants and bent close to my face and asked, "Was it good for you, too?"

Then he sat on the couch and acted as if nothing had happened.

As I struggled to dress myself, I glanced at my children's partially opened door to make sure they were not witnessing and noted no movement.

"You must leave now," I managed in a calm tone, realizing I was in the presence of an extremely dangerous man.

Luke looked a little surprised, mentioned offhandedly he was a bit tired, then rose, and headed to the door, which I opened quickly. Upon securing the lock, I rushed to the bathroom to scrub every inch of my defiled body in a hot shower until the water ran cold.

The following day, I dared not leave the house. The horrible scene on an unending loop in my brain continued to keep fresh tears in my eyes. My children softly asked what was wrong, afraid something they'd done brought on my dismay.

About one in the afternoon, the phone rang in my bedroom. Hoping it was Tammy, I hastened to answer it, but I froze in shock as I recognized my former boyfriend's voice. Marty started talking right away, sensing I might hang up the receiver.

"I heard there was a misunderstanding last night," he began.

"Misunderstanding?" I yelled. Then, remembering my children were in the living room watching television, I lowered my voice and shut my bedroom door.

"Luke raped me! Raped me with my children in the next room! What kind of guys do you call friends?"

"Well, he was upset, and he'd been drinking," Marty offered as a reason, not an excuse.

Suddenly, I heard my rapist's voice in the background. "Ask her what she's going to do," he said.

My mind whirred and lamely came up with, "He's a sheriff's deputy, for God's sake."

The rapist took the phone and breathed a threat. "If you say anything at all about this, your children might have a really bad accident."

I slammed the phone down, thinking: *This is what hell feels like.*

39

Moral Decisions

To make matters worse, the incident occurred while I wasn't on birth control pills. In recent years, my period arrived like clockwork at twenty-eight-day intervals.

Despair reared its ugly head as the days twenty-nine, thirty, thirty-one, and thirty-two dragged by. I phoned my sister in the Midwest and spilled my guts.

Lynn vowed to help in any way she could. As the first order of business, she stated that our parents could not be involved.

We knew from experience of their low tolerance for less-than-perfect behavior. They couldn't comprehend how their perceived perfect family plan somehow managed to allow continued havoc in their children's lives.

Lynn's first marriage was short-lived. Being a staunch believer in retaining her virginity for her one and only husband, a besotted suitor had married Lynn for the privilege, then left her after five tumultuous months for greener pastures. Our brother and I commiserated with her and kept Lynn buoyed as our parents reeled.

Her second marriage, occurring three months before the birth of her first child, found me again protectively by her side.

My sister's and my current plan began with me purchasing airline tickets to her area and her convincing her husband to allow us to visit for two weeks. Our four children's ages stair-stepped from four to seven years of age, and the cousins longed to get together anyway.

The loss of my first child, and a lingering sense of guilt at permitting her oxygen plug to be pulled, still haunted me, so couldn't I bear the thought of an abortion.

Lynn and I decided to find a new place near her for the children and me to live. I planned to give the unwanted child up for adoption and return to my former home after a reasonable amount of time, with no one the wiser.

The day following, spending half of my savings on the tickets, I got my period.

We enjoyed a lovely visit nevertheless, and I felt so much better after sharing my grief and fear with my trusted and non-judgmental sister.

I also made an appointment to have my fallopian tubes tied.

40

Rachael Resurrected

As I reunited with more divorced girlfriends, my social circle expanded. The late seventies, with disco dancing and the Women's Movement, blessed us with new freedoms. Widespread use of the birth control pill and low incidence of venereal disease encouraged promiscuity. Alcohol dulled our consciences.

Lifetimes of repressed sexual desires sought release in the country's return to a Roaring Twenties atmosphere. Strict religious morals took a backseat to a modern look at sexuality through wine-colored glasses and the sweet smell of marijuana.

At first shocked and timid, my increasing wine dependence led me by the hand to join the party.

My typical weekday morning included aspirin for an aching head, dressing for work, and dropping the children at school. From nine to three, I ran a real estate office for a successful broker, then retrieved the children, made dinner, drank a bottle of Hearty Burgundy, and went to bed.

In baseball and soccer season, I attended my son's games and chatted with the other parents in the fog, rain, and the occasional sunny day.

On the weekends, things were different. The partying, casual dating, and drinking increased.

One night, the phone rang as I slept. Fumbling with the phone, I murmured a hello and waited to hear a familiar friend on the line.

Instead, a smoky voice from my deep past called my name out twice. I struggled to sit in bed and asked tentatively, "Grandma Rachael?"

"Yes, my darlin', it's Grandma. How's my precious child? Are you well? How are your babies? I miss you so much."

I recognized her accent and heard tears in her voice. She sounded funny, like she'd been drinking, but as my curiosity overcame me, I responded, "Yes, Grandma, we're all fine. I miss you too. Why the call? Are you OK?"

Her response was an audible sob and a repetitive prayer, "I am so sorry, darlin', so very sorry. So sorry, so sorry. I missed all that time with you, and now it's too late. I'm oh, so sorry."

"It's OK," I answered. "I love you."

I don't know if she heard the last part, for the line went dead, and I never saw or heard from her again.

Not long after our final conversation, she fell in her kitchen and fractured a hip. She lay on the floor for two days before Aunt Billie found her, and checked her into the hospital, and then into an assisted living facility.

Grandma Rachael found a way to bribe the attendants to bring her booze, and when finally evicted, she spent the last days of her life with Aunt Billie.

Upon her death, one of her few meager possessions found its way to me. In a small padded envelope I found a short letter in her handwriting willing her small diamond wedding ring to me. It was taped to a piece of cardboard enclosed in the envelope.

I tried it on and wept as I conjured up memories of my namesake grandmother. She died unaware of the impact her stories and genes played in my exciting albeit dysfunctional life. Finally, she managed to share an intimacy with me.

It didn't last long.

As soon as her daughter, my Aunt Billie, traced the ring to me, she contacted my mother.

The resulting phone call to me from my mother begged a return of Rachael's ring to its supposedly rightful owner. Billie previously argued with her mother concerning her inherent right to the object, one Billie wished to pass on to her first daughter.

Grandma Rachael argued the ring was hers to dispose of, and she wished it to go to me, her eldest granddaughter. Unbeknownst to Aunt Billie, Rachael had used her persuasive skills to have a caregiver mail the ring to me.

The resolution of the family feud rested on my finger and tore at my heart.

My mother insisted the tenuous relationship between my father's family and his sister's demanded my return of the ring to Aunt Billie and left me no room for argument.

After much thought, and prayers aimed at Grandma Rachael, the massive rift to be caused by a small band of gold seemed to outweigh my grandmother's wishes to please me.

I appreciated beyond measure my grandmother's gesture, and treasured the gift, but sorrowfully sent the ring to my aunt and cousin.

41

Loneliness Beckons

Many months later, I learned from the local newspaper of a Parents Without Partners club in town and dared myself to attend a meeting. The well-known group sponsored various events for families, and others just for the adults. After joining the club, my small family and I enjoyed a summer of safe and fun-filled activities.

Eventually, I met a divorced man named Barry, who held joint custody of two young children. We were the same age, and his grey eyes and perfect teeth sparkled when he laughed. Barry worked at a non-profit organization and purported to believe in tough love when it came to raising youngsters.

As my son edged towards his teenage years, his mischievous ways escalated, and I felt my children needed a strong male presence in the house. Their father rarely saw them since marrying the younger woman, who kept him busy with weekend vacations in their sports car. In addition, I feared my son shared the same genetic predisposition for trouble that my brother did.

My drinking, although seemingly innocuous to me, bothered Barry. He didn't imbibe and seemed mysteriously spiritual in an unusual way. When confronted by any discord or difficult decision, he routinely stood erect, held one hand in the other, and closed his eyes—reminding me of a prayer moment.

My curiosity got the best of me, and I inquired as to what he did for religious practice. Barry had offhandedly spoken of his Methodist upbringing when I revealed myself a Catholic.

He confessed to practicing a "spiritual exercise" and gave it an exotic name. Barry told me he attended meetings twice a week and that the other participants varied in social status and occupations but mostly dealt in the healing arts.

The whole situation sounded a bit off-kilter to me, and I let the subject drop for the time being, but its siren's song pursued me.

42

Spiritually Off-Road

Over the coming weeks, we penciled in dates around Barry's spiritual duties and our children's activities.

My drinking routine, observed with concern by Barry, revealed itself as an addiction when I attempted to curtail it. Generations of genetic code had me by the throat.

Attempting a "one day at a time" approach proved difficult; the second day appeared nearly impossible. I was frightened, embarrassed, and humiliated at the thought of being an alcoholic.

Maybe I'm only a heavy drinker? I only drink wine. Doesn't that count for something?

Barry had disclosed his prior alcohol addiction to me. Now when he returned from one of his spiritual meetings and reported miraculous healings of addictions in his spiritual community, I quizzed him.

He provided additional background on the origin of the spiritual practice and its successful emigration to the United States.

Our present-day country's diverse societies included hippies, gurus, and cults. Upon sharing Barry's proclivity for an unusual spiritual practice with my parents, my mother immediately proclaimed him dangerous and warned me of his being a cult member.

Unfortunately, this alarm from my mother only made Barry and his congregation more alluring to the wild side of my personality. I requested Barry assist me in taking the first step to a possibly easy return to sobriety.

Soon I was invited to enter their private house of worship, a single-story rectangle building formerly used as a non-denominational church.

My preparatory meeting began at 10:00 a.m. inside a small office space, and I wasn't allowed to see any other portion of the building. I met with a different woman at each of three get-togethers.

Alisha, probably in her twenties, was tall and slender while Michaela seemed to be in her seventies and wore her grey hair in a casual bun. Celeste, my favorite, smiled all the time like an angel. All of them appeared gentle, kind, and quietly spiritual, akin to cloistered nuns, I thought.

The women used these meetings to take stock of my spiritual status. No points were allocated for affiliation with an organized religion. The questions pertained to my relationship with God and how often we communicated. What was my concept of the Afterlife and what awaited me there? This was soul-level stuff and intensely intimate.

With my sincerity affirmed by my interviewers, I was instructed to return on Thursday evening with Barry to join the others and take the next initiation step. I received instructions to wear a long unrestricting skirt, a modest long-sleeved blouse, and a light sweater if I needed additional warmth.

Barry and I drove together on the appointed evening so he could attend the men's prayer meeting and I could commence my apprenticeship with the women. I received no explanation for the sexes praying in separate rooms.

Clad in a long, pale-blue denim skirt and a chaste long-sleeve blouse, I blended with the other quiet women who entered mid-building and veered off to the right end of the corridor.

The silent men, wearing regular trousers and shirts, turned left in the corridor and headed to a room marked "Auditorium" behind closed double doors.

It all felt so solemn and mysterious that the hairs prickled at the back of my neck and on my arms.

Near the double doors leading into the women's prayer room, I was met by Celeste, who put her finger to her lips to stifle my greeting. She used her right hand to indicate a claustrophobia-inducing coat closet with a folding chair pushed up against one wall and waved me to the seat.

At the conclusion of my gentle grilling a week before, I had received permission to sit in the coat closet outside the women's prayer room. I promised to sit there until told to leave and was firmly instructed to make no sound, no matter what I heard beyond the doors.

This whole experience seemed thrilling and otherworldly, and I could hardly wait until their session of prayer commenced.

To be totally honest, I fully intended to bolt from the quasi-cell and hide out in Barry's car if anything weird spooked me, promise or no promise.

43

Taste Of Heaven

For what seemed like an exceptionally long time, nothing happened. I had been instructed not to wear any jewelry, including my watch, and there wasn't a clock in the closet, of course.

I began to think the whole thing was an elaborate prank as the "new kid" in me recalled the memory of my cramped school locker in junior high. It seemed only a bit smaller than this darn coat-filled closet I found myself in now.

Just as I attempted to stand amidst the hanging coats to ease out into the hall, I heard the rustling of skirts through the cracks between the double doors. I dropped like a stone back onto the metal chair with a bit of thud.

Oops!

Be quiet! I admonished myself. *Don't move!* I felt a nervous giggle bubble up and covered my mouth to stifle it.

Then, simultaneously, without an audible signal, one female voice rose in a wordless song, another lifted her voice in some strange language, and yet another praised God as if at a county fair revival. The singing and praying intensified, without any rhyme or reason.

The sounds of the voices seemed to move as if their owners were circulating around some large dance floor, without order or purpose.

The angelic songs and joyful prayers resonated like a powerful echo down the lengthy hallway as the men's voices rushed up the hall like a cataclysm to mesh and mingle with the female chorus.

Caught somewhere in the middle of this tremendous spiritual energy, I felt as if the air was forced from my lungs and I gasped repeatedly to regain it.

After maybe fifteen minutes, to my dismay and as if on cue, the mixture of heavenly voices ceased simultaneously. I thought I'd gone deaf.

Confused, yet joyful and energized, I awaited Celeste's signal to permit my re-entry to the hall. After peering in at me and searching my face, she smiled. Returning her smile, I left my unholy closet as Celeste said, "See you next week. Same time, same closet."

Back in the car, Barry asked if I enjoyed the experience, and I could only nod my approval. My mind and spirit fought internally for explanations, but I knew one thing for certain. This was my first sweet taste of heaven in a world where I had often choked on mouthfuls of hell.

44

Welcome Invitation

Never before had I looked forward to spending an evening in a closet, but I did so now. *How long will I have to wait until I can join the joyful women in the mysterious space behind the heavenly gates?*

The week dragged on, and I attempted to gain information from Barry, but his constant refrain of "You'll just have to be patient. Wait and see!" angered me.

Patience was not my middle name or even a distant cousin. I noticed that a few glasses of wine did nothing to ease the conflict in my soul, but I drank them anyway.

On the appointed evening, clad in my denim skirt and white blouse, I tapped my foot impatiently as Barry searched for the car keys.

As soon as Barry parked, I leapt from the vehicle and rushed up the three steps to the interior, turned right to join the women's parade, and slipped into my hidey-hole.

When Celeste espied me, she smiled, then slowly closed the tall doors to the sacred space after the last of the ladies entered.

This time, I closed my eyes, attempted to quiet my inner self, and calmly waited.

As the first clear, high note soared, I felt my soul leap with it. Tears of joy filled my eyes and rolled down my smiling face. I didn't want the experience to end.

My eyes flew open when all sounds ceased, and I uncharacteristically sat patiently awaiting my release.

At last, Celeste stood in the doorway but asked me to stay until the others departed. When she returned, Celeste invited me to come the following day to be formally inducted into the community. She explained it would occur during a prayer session consisting of the four of us.

Hold on! I thought. *What kind of commitment am I making here? What changes in my life must I make? Do I have to quit drinking cold turkey?*

These questions flooded my brain, but my inner Voice urged me to calm down and to just ask, "What time?"

45

Dancing With God

Wearing my now-familiar uniform, Barry and I drove in silence into unchartered territory. It was almost three o'clock, and the sun shone brightly.

He attempted to stifle his excitement while I wished I'd taken a bit more time to think through this life-changing event. I tend to make snap decisions based on emotion rather than logic, but this decision seemed to have the additional unmeasured ingredient of God's will.

My stomach was full of butterflies, or maybe angels; I couldn't be sure.

Barry walked me to the corridor, and I advanced to the women's section without looking back at him.

Celeste, Alisha, and Michaela met me at the double doors. They sensed my conflicted emotional vibes and smiled kindly. Taking a deep, shaky breath, I followed them inside and heard the doors close behind me.

The room was exceptionally large, rectangular in shape, and had a well-worn hardwood floor. I noticed the old-fashioned tan shades covering the tall windows were pulled to the sills, so the room was dimly lit.

Since the women began removing their socks and shoes, I did the same.

In response to my name being called by Celeste, I stood up and reached out to join the intimate circle formed by their clasped hands. A soft squeeze greeted each of my hands, and as I looked up, I noticed they had all closed their eyes, so I shut mine.

Celeste began in a firm voice, “Rachael, you are about to experience God in a way you have never imagined. You must trust that God loves you and would never harm you.”

I was startled when this beginning sentence resurrected in me deep-seated sorrow, disappointment, and memories of near despair. I let out a sob and hung my head in confusion and doubt.

I attempted to release my hands, but the women held firm and whispered comforting sounds and phrases like a mother uses to soothe a troubled young child.

Michaela’s tone was instructional when she told me, “First, we will separate and sit on the bench along the wall, where we will close our eyes and let all thoughts drift out of our minds. Quiet your inner self and let your soul rest.

“Alisha will rise and walk to the floor when it is time to do so, and we will join her, leaving space between us. Close your eyes and do not open them until the activities cease at her command. Then, quietly return to your seat at the bench and wait for Alisha to stand and end the session."

I wanted to turn and run from this place, far and fast. God seemed to be breathing down my neck, and I couldn't hide from Him. No longer some faraway impersonal deity, I sensed Him lovingly holding me in His hands.

After disengaging, we walked to the plain wooden bench and sat down. As instructed, I closed my eyes and placed my hands in my lap. I'd heard of the practice of meditation and assumed they meant for me to attempt it now. I really didn't know its ins and outs, so I decided to fake it.

Quieting my mind was laughable, but I kept my smirk to myself and just sat there.

After about fifteen minutes of listening to the birds beyond the windows and enjoying the cool room, I began nodding off. Gratefully, I heard the rustle of skirts and the padding of bare feet and jerked to attention. I rose with opened eyes, found a spot some distance from the women, and shut my eyes again.

As a clear, sweet anthem rose from the women, I felt someone behind me press on the backside of my knees. Gently, though firmly, the pressure caused me to ease to the floor and into a kneeling position.

In a rational state of mind, I assumed one of the women had moved behind me to encourage this position of traditional Catholic worship to make me more comfortable with my praying.

So, I prayed. It was a monologue on my part, as usual, but my standard Our Father and Hail Mary droned on in my mind.

Suddenly, I heard a male voice clearly say, “Listen!”

Forgetting the rules, I looked about for the forbidden male and attempted to rise from the floor. The same firm touch that urged me to my knees now pressed on my shoulder.

The women continued singing and added words of praise as they danced and swirled about the floor, eyes closed yet not bumping into each other.

There was no visible hand on my shoulder or male in the room. I reasoned that I should be spooked at this point but only felt peaceful and safe.

Relaxing to my former position, the pressure on my shoulder lifted, and I listened intently to silence until Alisha finally uttered a simple word and all activity ceased.

We returned to the bench, closed our eyes, and rested for about ten minutes, then Alisha rose, and we followed her to the door and into the hall.

The three circled round me and asked how I felt and what had transpired.

I related my tale of being pushed to my knees and being told to listen to silence. Not overly exciting, but accurate.

Michaela laughed, and the other two exchanged knowing looks.

"Good start!" said Celeste. "Every time gets better. We all need a little purification to start the process. Stick with it. You won't be sorry."

Alisha added, "See you on Thursday."

This was the beginning of my unique experience as the "new kid" in the spiritual, but not religious, realm.

46

My Constant Companion

The Voice, for want of a better term, seems like a child's "invisible friend." I learned to listen to it when it crept into my head at an early age. This internal presence feels like my conscience, a guardian angel, or maybe the Holy Spirit.

As I became an adult, I challenged It, fearing I might be on the verge of schizophrenia.

However, when I shared my fear with Alisha, Celeste, and Michaela, they attested to its validity, citing their own communication with the Voice. They claimed It to be the Voice of God and encouraged me to intensify my listening skills.

Having always conversed with my Guardian Angel, and even Jesus, since my early childhood, the leap to conversing with God was an easy one.

My continued semiweekly interactions with the women's group brought me joy and peace. I willingly accepted the pressure to my knees during the first few sessions and was pleasantly surprised to find myself standing throughout on the fourth.

Gradually, other movements, as simple as raising my arms in a praising position or swaying from side to side, occurred spontaneously. As I gave myself over to the holy energy, my voice joined the others singing words I did not understand, reminding me of charismatics "speaking in tongues."

As time progressed, I grew more comfortable with my personal interaction with God and one evening asked Him a question while awaiting our session to commence.

I told God He knew me well enough to know that I got bored easily and, quite frankly, the idea of dying and going to heaven just to sing old praise songs with a bunch of angels for all eternity seemed, well, boring.

When our session commenced, instead of being moved to sing or dance about, I stood stock still with my hands comfortably raised. A rush of ecstasy so overwhelmed me with unspeakable joy that I thought my heart would explode! Tears of pure happiness ran down my face as my entire being vibrated like a living song.

I desired to bask there in God's presence forever and was devastated when Alisha came and laid her hand on my shoulder after everyone else had finished, and the heavenly sensation ceased. Time had stood still for me, although twenty minutes had passed for the others.

God had blessed me with a preview of heaven, and I couldn't wait to return to His home again to spend eternity in such bliss. It was as far from boring as a soul could get!

On the nights we gathered, no alcohol, caffeine, or recreational drugs could be used on that day. The spiritual practice required it, and everyone respected the rule, including me.

Missing my wine twice a week never bothered me once I began worshiping God in this manner. I found my desire for alcohol gradually lessened and then disappeared—without any effort on my part. It just stopped appealing to me.

I ceased drinking alcohol for two years.

47

Yes Or No?

After many months of dating, Barry suggested we join our families by getting married. The idea didn't appeal to me, and the divorce with Mike still brought unpleasant consequences. In addition, our combined children were not warming to our relationship or to each other and argued constantly.

The spiritual practice I had adopted offered a formal method of asking questions of God and receiving His answers.

Barry suggested I consult Celeste about the process. She might agree to assist me in deciding whether to marry him or not.

The upshot of the short session proved only partially helpful.

At their special meeting, one of the ladies clearly felt a heaviness and gloom at a marriage with Barry; a second saw me like Peter walking across the water to Jesus, indicating my need for faith; and the final woman said the marriage would be difficult, but not marrying Barry would make my life more difficult than if I accepted the union.

Better than having no advice at all, I agreed to the marriage, as I feared what might have transpired if I chose not to unite with Barry.

Our simple wedding in my parish church, with the small reception at the remodeled schoolhouse, was uneventful. However, it wasn't long before my children hated him, and his children hated me. It was a mess.

I had full custody of my children, and he shared custody with his unpleasant and spiteful ex-wife. Half the week we shared two children, and the other half of the week, there were four.

Barry sold his home and put his half of the proceeds in the bank. He and his children moved into my compact three-bedroom apartment, a post-divorce upgrade to my family's first tiny duplex. Six people in such a small place exacerbated the chaos and lack of privacy.

I worked a six-hour day job and was attending night school to become a real estate agent. My shopping and dinner preparation happened in between the two activities. Housework and laundry needed my attention on weekends.

With the extra family, I was exhausted and short-tempered. Chris and Lauren toed the line, but Barry's youngsters were wild and spoiled. Their "New Age" mom did not believe in discipline, only loving direction.

As her four-year-old son crawled across my family's dinner table to reach the salt shaker one evening, I firmly picked up his rude self and placed him back in his chair. I directed him to ask for the salt shaker, with a "please" attached, in the future.

When Barry's seven-year-old daughter didn't get her way, she would stomp up the stairs to her shared room and slam the door with all her might. One evening, I stomped up the stairs after her, opened her door, and calmly told her she was not to pull that stunt again. Her widened eyes told me she was not familiar with correction. The use of that stunt ceased.

One of our house rules required all residents to take personal items into their bedrooms before settling down to television. Coats, shoes, paperwork, and toys were included in the edict.

On my college school nights, Barry was responsible for supervising the children's bath schedules and enforcing the "no-littering-in-the-hall" rule.

One late night, dragging home after a difficult day at work and fixing the family dinner before rushing off to night school, I entered the home after ten o'clock to find an unwelcome circus.

I stood transfixed as I noted the strip-tease scene of clothes dropped to the floor the entire length of the hall, mingled with schoolbooks and toys. Unbathed children shrieked and teased one another while Barry relaxed on the couch, watching MTV on a blaring television set.

I inhaled deeply, hung my coat in the hall closet, and set my purse on the kitchen counter. I then proceeded down the hall, picking up every item until my arms were full. Without a word, and with multiple pairs of eyes upon me, I crossed the now silent room, opened the kitchen trash cover, and stuffed everything inside.

Barry leapt from the couch, shouting, "We had spaghetti for dinner, and the trash can is full of sauce. Those new jackets will be ruined!"

His children bemoaned the soiling of their school papers and toys. Chris and Lauren scampered upstairs and wisely disappeared. Their items were safely in their rooms, having learned that rule as preschoolers.

When the hubbub subsided, I calmly reminded them of the house rule concerning such things and made my way upstairs. Thereafter, I never faced another disorderly homecoming.

Soon after that event, Barry and I bought a larger home together to relieve some of the tension resulting from the close quarters. Barry had some money left from the sale of his former home, and so did I.

However, as the four children grew older, the chaos increased. My teenagers were angry with Barry's increasingly strict rules pertaining to homework and curfews. Barry's children could apparently do no wrong and were only occasionally rebuked by their father.

When Chris and Lauren enjoyed a rare visit with their father and stepmother, they were offered beer and marijuana and stayed out late without consequences. My children resented Barry's demeaning attitude toward them and threatened to decamp to their father's domicile, leaving me to endure Barry and his kids alone.

48

Strike Two

After three years of a disastrous marriage, Barry suffered a nervous breakdown, for want of a better medical term.

We still belonged to our alternative spiritual community and attended group meetings twice a week, but Barry started abusing the practice by performing it on his own, at all hours of the day and night.

It became an addiction and slowly untethered him from reality.

He began hearing a voice from "God" instructing him to do unusual things.

"God" told Barry to quit his job, so he did this without consulting me, leaving only my meager income to provide for our family of six.

Barry said "God" directed him to work with a local shoe company, but when Barry told the store owner that his background was in office management, the man sent him on his way.

Awaiting "God's" next move, Barry took to sitting in a low beach chair in our living room, practicing on his ukulele. It was surreal and terrifying to come home day after day to off-key Hawaiian music. I prayed he'd recover his senses, but the days went by without any improvement.

Since Barry wouldn't see a therapist, I felt no choice but to sever the relationship. Our finances would soon take a dangerous turn with our single income, and I feared getting deeper in debt.

I told Barry of my plans to divorce him, hoping only slightly he would snap out of whatever funk he was in.

The next day Barry handed me an envelope with my full name neatly printed on the outside and a typed letter inside. He asked that I read it alone in my room.

The letter indicated that Barry had spoken to "God" about my intentions, and "God" had made it clear to him that, should I insist on a divorce, Barry was to kill me.

Shaking with fear and anger, I returned to the living room to face Barry, but he wouldn't look up from his chair, only continued strumming the damned ukulele.

After sending my children to their dad's house for a week, I planned my escape. Grandma Rachael was often on my mind.

I easily got a restraining order at the courthouse by showing the clerk Barry's threatening letter. My sister served the order on Barry the same afternoon. Lynn told me he had taken the paper after pausing on the ukulele, read the order, dropped it to the floor next to his chair, and continued with his plunking.

Thankfully, Barry disappeared overnight, and I immediately changed the locks.

My sister helped me transfer Barry's possessions to the garage, and she phoned him to set up a meeting to collect them.

With a previous divorce for practice, and the need to conserve resources, I drew up our petition papers by myself and presented them to the court.

Our marriage was short-lived, and we had no children together. I didn't want any support and suggested we split the meager assets evenly between us. The house was on the market for sale, and any proceeds would be split as well.

Nonetheless, the divorce hearing was a debacle, and my husband argued with the judge over every part of my petition. Barry's arrogant and rude outbursts wore on the judge's nerves, but Barry pressed on.

Although Barry was the least athletic person I knew, it didn't deter him from buying expensive sports equipment, using money from our meager budget. He would see a snazzy tennis racket, or regulation basketball, and purchase it on a whim.

When Barry returned from a game or two, complaining of tennis elbow or sore knees, he'd confine the equipment to a corner of our garage.

Consequently, when dividing up our personal belongings on my proposed divorce decree, his column included the expensive sports collection. Barry squawked to the judge that half of those items were mine because of the California law of joint property.

The judge shot him down with a searing gaze and a generous tap of the gavel.

My soon-to-be ex-husband spoke up again, alleging I had insisted the two of us eat dinner out at least once a week during our marriage, against his wishes. Barry demanded to be reimbursed for each of the meals, produced all the offending dining receipts with a flourish, and informed the judge of the grand total.

The judge, exasperated by Barry's pettiness, asked him if he had eaten these meals with me at the time of the forced outings. Barry reluctantly confessed doing so. The judge said that Barry already had half of the expense in his stomach, and crashed the gavel down loudly on his desk, adding a clear announcement that everything in my petition was agreeable to the court.

Waving to the deputy sheriff at the door, the judge glared at Barry and told him to remove himself immediately from the courtroom. As the officer escorted Barry from the room, and the judge gave me a thumbs-up gesture, I said to myself, "My, that went well!"

Gathering my paperwork, I collected my stamped court approval certificate and smiled broadly for the first time in years.

A few weeks later, Barry rang the doorbell of my new apartment, and my heart beat in triple time with fear. I inquired through the open, yet chained, door as to what he wanted.

Barry reported that he had found a box of my belongings among his own and was returning photo albums and other personal effects.

I instructed him to deposit the box at the porch and to step back into the parking lot, which he did.

Opening the door part way, I glanced at the suspicious box, and then at Barry.

He raised his voice so that I could hear him and said, "God told me to sell all my possessions and move to Guam. I leave on Thursday."

I sent a hasty prayer of thanksgiving heavenward and answered, "Oh, good luck."

He turned away and entered his car with one last comment, "I'm out of your life forever."

"Amen," I whispered under my breath.

Since his daughter still attended high school with mine, we later learned that "God" changed His mind as Barry awaited his flight to Guam and rerouted him to Oxnard, where Barry's mom lived. She took pity on him since he had sold all his possessions. We lost track of him after that last little bit of information. I still have nightmares about Barry and his children.

That marriage and family relationship was the most hellish five continuous years of my life, but I will concede that if Barry hadn't been a part of the family, my teenage son might have gone down a darker path.

Barry's strict rules kept Chris from spending time with an unruly crowd in the evening hours and pushed him to attain higher grades. I had been unsuccessful on either front before Barry joined our family. Time spent on education rather than getting into trouble proved imperative to Chris' success in getting his college degrees in upcoming years.

Were it not for Barry, I might never have found my additional spiritual practice or reaped the benefits of its experiences, which invaluably deepened my relationship with my loving heavenly Father.

God, and "God," works in strange ways indeed.

49

Starting Over

My teens and I relocated into a small condominium while I continued working six hours a day and attended night classes to earn my real estate license.

When Chris turned sixteen, he asked to purchase a used automobile with money from a fund set up by his paternal grandparents. He and Lauren were in high school, and his having a car would benefit me, too.

Chris and his best friend scoured the local paper and discovered two possibilities. His friend chose one of the cars, so my son pursued the other. I contacted the car's owner and said I needed to have the vehicle checked out by my mechanic prior to any offer to purchase.

The appointment was arranged, and a gentleman came to my office to drop off his car. When Rick walked through the door, a beautiful smile lit up his face. I was impressed not only with his suit and tie, short haircut, and incredibly blue eyes, but his reaction to me. It warmed my heart. We clicked.

When the auto proved sound, I asked Rick to reduce the price since I was a single mom with two kids. He countered with, “I’ll lower the price if you’ll have a drink with me.”

It was a win-win. I agreed; one drink only—and it would be non-alcoholic.

My son’s seemingly inconsequential choice of cars introduced me to my number one soulmate.

50

Prince Charming

Over his glass of fine red wine and my 7-Up on the rocks, Rick confided that his recent divorce coincided with the first big step toward his chosen career as a general manager of a large food-producing facility.

Due to Rick's desire to achieve a higher level than his father did in the same field, Rick revealed that he was the youngest GM ever hired in his well-known company's lengthy history.

At eighteen, Rick had approached his dad, hoping to receive financial support for higher education, but with Rick's four younger brothers lined up behind him, it wasn't possible.

Rick said, "Dad, I'm hoping to go to college next fall."

His father, Herbert, replied, "Son, I won't stand in your way."

With his recent hiring, Rick received an upscale company car for his use, thus prompting his desire to sell his old Toyota to my son. Rick used funds from his bountiful salary to update his wardrobe and embarked on his hobby of wine collecting.

Rick felt his life was finally coming together after long years of college and working odd jobs to pay for his education. He gladly immersed himself in long hours at the facility and kept his personal secretary hopping with correspondence.

Rick was thirty-nine years old, six months older than I was.

With two years of sobriety under my belt and no desire for alcohol, Rick and I discovered a glitch in our seemingly perfect relationship. Rick loved wine.

Having downplayed the reasons for my alcohol-free lifestyle, Rick assumed I only needed to be introduced to an upgrade to Gallo Hearty Burgundy, my prior drug of choice.

Our first date was a doozy.

Rick escorted me into a cozy country vineyard restaurant featuring a monthly pairing of choice varietals with a seven-course dining experience.

Way out of my league, I vowed to only pretend to drink, when the first of many glasses of wine arrived with a flourish. As one gourmet delicacy after another beckoned to me, the temptation for just a sip of the accompanying fragrant liquids won out.

Lordy, it was a long, hard fall from abstinence, and as Rick steered me to the car at the end of the evening, he remarked on my inability to keep up with his seasoned tolerance.

“You just need some practice,” he reasoned as I fought the urge to gag.

I think even Grandma Rachael would have counseled me differently.

51

Our Forever Song

Rick and Me

Even though Rick had a lot on his plate with his new job, he found time to woo me.

Rick treated me to nice restaurants where we'd share a bottle of fine wine and eat sumptuous cuisine. Rick had been raised in a middle-class family and hungered for the good life.

With his generous salary, he acquired a taste for expensive shirts and soft leather business shoes. Rick's build fit perfectly into a suit and tie, and he always looked most comfortable dressed like a successful businessman.

He inherited, or acquired, a soft drawl from his Southern-born mother, who was the epitome of a "lady." Rick's voice felt pleasant and comforting, and he even sounded polite when he argued, which wasn't often.

For a surprise, Rick whisked me off to the mountains one long weekend, not revealing our destination until we pulled off the highway. From our room in an upscale lodge, our view of Mt. Shasta was breathtaking.

The few invigorating days of walking in meadows, exploring the town for quirky restaurants, and browsing through shops gave us time for revealing ourselves. Hand in hand, we laughed, dreamed, and shared companionable silences.

A popular song at that time was "Heaven" by Bryan Adams. We enjoyed hearing it frequently on our car radio.

One moonlit night in our suite, the sound of it lulled us as we lay in each other's arms. Rick whispered, "That's our song."

"Oh, once in your life you find someone
Who will turn your world around
Bring you up when you're feelin' down
And baby, you're all that I want
When you're lyin' here in my arms
I'm finding it hard to believe
We're in heaven."

Those romantic words eventually became a reality.

52

Life With Rick

Rick not only strove for professional excellence; he continually encouraged me to take a leap of faith in myself and start my own real estate firm.

Having promised Rick I'd make an honest move in this direction, I reluctantly considered my first client, a wealthy friend from high school who shared his dream of purchasing multiple rental units. He requested my immediate assistance and offered me a generous commission cut to do so.

Rick, playing cheerleader and guide, formulated a plan for a resignation from my current employer, and the transfer of my real estate license, so I could work on my own from home.

The plan took little time to implement, and soon my first client, Roger, jumped into my car to begin hunting. Word of mouth brought me his investor brothers, my parents' friends, and other locals.

I attended a seminar on marketing at the local telephone company and crafted a plain yet clever Yellow Pages advertisement to attract out-of-towners. It showcased the name of my real estate company, my smiling image in color, and the words: *I cater to small investors.*

Since all the other companies in my genre boasted numerous staff and multiple offices, my company consisting of one person attracted clients seeking a personal touch.

Almost every time I received a call from someone answering the ad, they'd start with "I'm looking at your friendly face and I'm a small investor."

I'd reply seriously, "Are you under 5'6"?" Some people got the joke right away and belly laughed; others took a couple of minutes. It always broke the ice, and I reeled them in.

My sister's best friend inherited her father's real estate office and used the small building to work from. After some finagling, she sub-let a desk in her space to me, and since our targeted markets differed, competition for clients didn't complicate our association.

I reveled in the new-found freedom of owning my own business and taking charge of my life. My debt to Rick for encouraging me and believing in me could never be repaid.

Over the next eleven years, my business grew steadily, and I secured two priceless employees to assist me: my sister, Lynn, and my daughter, Lauren, when she was fresh from college.

Working six days a week brought me purpose and joy, not to mention financial security and pride of accomplishment.

With Rick at my side, life felt perfect.

After our first year of dating, Rick and I decided to purchase a large home together. Since Chris and Lauren still lived with me then, each of us claimed one of the four bedrooms for propriety's sake.

Rick surprised me with a beautiful diamond ring for Christmas. Neither of us wanted marriage in the near future, so the ring also served as a token to satisfy his boss and my mother, who thought Rick a "perfect catch."

The conservative company Rick worked for believed married men to be more dependable and socially acceptable, and his superior often quizzed him on our wedding date. I didn't want to risk another unfortunate stepfather situation, although Rick was perfect with my children. Our plan to marry would take place well after my children left for college as fledgling adults.

As a result of the formal engagement, we spent more time with Rick's folks, who lived an easy forty-minute drive from us. His dad, Herbert, and his mom, Beth, were a contrast in breeding, personality, and style.

I loved his mom for her sweet disposition and calm, friendly demeanor. Herbert was an Irish-flavored scallywag. Blessedly, all five of their sons took after their mother in their temperaments and manners. However, they also received their dad's quick wit and mischievous inclinations in spades.

This blend of unpredictable gentlemen sought to incorporate me into their family and easily captivated me. My acceptance as a target/sister took place at our initial meeting at their annual Thanksgiving dinner.

Nervously, I entered the seemingly normal family gathering and was rapidly introduced to Rick's mom and dad, four brothers, two sisters-in-law, and a nephew, Marcus. After a minimum of chit-chat, we gathered at the formal dining room table, extended to its full length.

Only Rick and I were served a glass of wine from the bottle Rick brought, the rest were non-imbibers.

Beth displayed her finest china and silverware and had heaped turkey, mashed potatoes, homemade rolls, salad, and condiments in an orderly and enticing fashion. Everything looked wonderful and smelled great! My mouth watered as I participated in dipping into the steady progression of yummy-looking dishes.

"To the right. To the right." the boys chanted, knowing the rules by heart.

When the passing ceased, the family looked to Herbert and they all bowed their heads. The patriarch invoked God's blessing on the food and family. The six-year-old nephew added, "Dig in!"

Intent on our feast, I picked up my knife and fork and proceeded to cut apart a small slice of turkey.

Something caught my eye.

Somehow, a housefly had attached itself to my fork, and I shuddered. Dropping the fork unobtrusively to the napkin in my lap, I attempted to wipe it off, but it remained.

Hearing a chuckle, I looked across the table to see one of Rick's brothers, Fred, holding his hand over his mouth in a failed attempt to keep from bursting into laughter.

Beth looked up and caught Fred's impolite outburst and then turned her measured gaze on me. I held the offensive fork up and smiled weakly. At this, the rest of the brothers, including Rick, laughed at my expense.

Their mother quieted the outburst with the raising of one hand. "Fred," she sighed, "I requested that you be polite to Rick's guest and that included no shenanigans with your trick fork."

Holding high the offensive tool, I joined in the laughter and sweetly added, "I'll get you for this, Fred."

I was officially one of the unruly gang.

53

Chris

A staunch believer in the benefits of higher education, Rick generously volunteered to contribute half of Chris' and Lauren's tuition and living expenses when they entered college.

Our first higher-education experience was with Chris as he was accepted to a university in Southern California.

My dear son inherited a few too many of my wild brother's genes in addition to a plethora of my father's intelligent and logical brain cells.

Chris managed to get a four-year degree at a respectable college in "only" seven years. In his fifth and sixth years, he appeared to be majoring in "fraternity."

Rick relentlessly encouraged Chris to attain a degree, explaining this certificate would not only secure more upscale opportunities for employment but encourage him to stretch his mind.

Because Chris merited admittance to Mensa in his first year of high school, Rick and I vowed to pay Chris' basic college expenses if he retained a passing grade point average. Never exerting himself more than absolutely necessary, Chris maintained a solid C, and thereby ensured our long-term backing.

After we purchased a run-down house near the school for Chris to reside in, he was responsible for finding additional roommates to help subsidize its mortgage. Student housing was woefully difficult to find, and Rick and I felt better knowing Chris had a roof over his head, and we'd know where to find him.

Other than irritating neighbors with their parties, and lack of proper yard maintenance, the mixture of tenants sufficed. Two years later, Lauren joined the household, and the place finally got cleaned.

One evening, Chris crossed the line and got ratted out by his friend who called me with concern. Someone brought a small amount of cocaine to their house, and Chris decided to give it a try.

I went ballistic! His beer drinking was already a concern of mine; drugs just couldn't be tolerated. I phoned, catching him off guard with my announcement of knowing his secret.

He admitted a single use of the drug and swore never to repeat the offense.

"Never mind the promise," I said firmly. "You and your friends will be receiving a thirty-day written notice to vacate, and your funding stops now. I'm living on jelly sandwiches and wearing old clothes so you can have a decent education. There is no way I'm going to be throwing my hard-earned money away for you to buy drugs."

I hung up the phone. Rick gave me a thumbs-up gesture and we awaited Chris' return call, which came immediately.

After his groveling, and a multitude of insistent promises, I agreed to one more chance. To the best of my knowledge, and according to spy reports, he stuck to beer after that incident.

54

Working Couple

When it was Lauren's turn to leave the nest, she decided to join her brother's dorm-style household in Southern California.

As my teenagers began morphing into young adults, their father and his wife found them more tolerable. They now welcomed Chris and Lauren to stay with them for school breaks. Our oversized house seemed cavernous with just Rick and I living there.

We both worked long hours most days but saved each Friday evening for date night. The rest of the week I cooked our dinner meals, and we enjoyed a glass of wine each night from his extensive fine wine collection. Our financial situation allowed me a long-awaited freedom from money worries for the first time in my adult life

Thank God, my full and stable life no longer required vast amounts of alcohol numbing, and my drinking remained moderate.

My dependable sister/assistant manager offered to free up some of my workload. I longed for relaxing weekend travel with Rick, but his nose was riveted to the grindstone. I grew more disappointed each time his multiple obligations disrupted our few opportunities to spend time together as a loving couple, and I missed the fun and intimacy.

For one such romantic adventure, I purchased a black lace nightie for an appetizer and lay it provocatively in the back of our getaway car over my luggage. Without so much as a second glance, Rick stacked a pile of work file folders and his briefcase alongside my things.

I had been holding the door open for Rick as he added his overnight necessities and watched in shock at the implications for the weekend.

Raising my voice, I said, "Oh, no you don't! This is a quality-time trip for us, Rick! Either you take that work crap out of the car, or I'll retrieve the nightie and you can go by yourself!"

"I have an important report due on Monday," he reasoned to his unreasonable fiancée.

I moved to the other side of the car and bent in to retrieve my belongings.

"Don't," he said and gathered up his briefcase and files and lugged them back into our home. Rick returned to the car, indicated that I should close the back car door and get into the front seat with basic hand signals, and slid into the driver's side.

After a while, it wasn't worth the effort.

Fortuitously, a colleague of mine asked me a *huge* favor: to sponsor a college Japanese student during the summer while he took an English-speaking class at our local university.

Toni handed me a stack of the male students' photos and asked me to pick one. After fanning through dozens of mugshots of seeming criminals, my initial negative reaction waffled when a whimsical picture caused me to chuckle.

I held up a photo of a darling young man flirting with the camera. Kneeling on one knee, he held his chin in his right hand and grinned. The name on the back was Tanoshi.

I reluctantly accepted the photo and told Toni I'd check with Rick for a final decision. My spirits rose as I read the accompanying paperwork detailing duties and perks of hosting one of the hundred young people involved in a well-established student exchange program.

The thought of having a buddy from a foreign culture to take on field trips and introduce to American life buoyed me.

Rick realized my dearth of his attention and my craving to socialize more often. He complied with my request, as long as he wasn't pulled from his duties.

The deal was sealed, and I anticipated upcoming adventures. As it turned out, Tanoshi, Rick, and I became forever friends.

I would even save Tanoshi's life.

55

World War II Rewrite

Tanoshi and His Bride with Rick and Me

My parents were horrified!

"Why in the world would you shelter the enemy in your own home?" demanded my dad.

"After what they did to your father?" Mom all but shouted.

"Huh?" I managed, shocked at my dad's refusal to even examine the contents of the manila envelope with Tanoshi's picture or the brochures for the student exchange program.

An innocuous decision on my part promulgated a dialogue of some of the long-buried war experiences, which had never before been revealed to my siblings or me.

On the night of Tanoshi 's arrival, following his fourteen-hour flight and a lengthy bus trip from the airport, he stumbled into Rick's and my kitchen. Tanoshi proceeded to dump his heavy luggage unceremoniously on the floor.

Then Tanoshi pulled out a jumble of papers from his jacket, smoothed them onto the dining table, took a chair, and gestured for us to join him.

Surprised at the formality, we sat and waited.

In broken but mostly discernible English, Tanoshi pointed at a map of Japan and said, "This Osaka. I live here with palents."

My mind did a double-take at his use of an "l" for the "r" in parents. Tanoshi and the other Japanese students switched "l" and "r" on a regular basis. I'd get used to the "accent" with time.

"Yes, I see," said Rick seriously.

"Mmm," responded Tanoshi. Moving his finger to another spot on the map, he proclaimed, "This Kyoto. Glandpalents live here."

Boring! I thought. *Where is the personality promised in this kid's photo?*

Much to Rick's dismay, I jumped in.

"Where does Godzilla live?" I queried innocently.

Rick intercepted with a, "Now, Rach, Tanoshi is probably tired and..."

"Godzirra?" clarified Tanoshi.

"Mmm," I affirmed.

Tanoshi kept eye contact with me as he dragged his finger across the map and plopped it in the middle of the ocean, seemingly thousands of miles away from Japan.

"Way out there?" I shrieked. "How does he get to Japan so often?"

Without a hint of a smile, he said, "Take big step."

"Mmm," was my serious response as our eyes twinkled at each other.

We bonded.

Rick put his head in his hands and sighed.

56

Host Mother

In a nutshell, Tanoshi and I milked every minute out of his rapidly passing time with us. It was as if we were strange soulmates, and we felt like an instant family. He called me "host mother," so I played along and referred to him as "host son."

Tanoshi was fascinated that I attended Mass every morning after dropping him at college for his weekday classes, and we discussed the differences in our religious beliefs. He professed to be a Buddist atheist or some strange combination of foreign terms muddled in the translation.

One day, on our drive home, he inquired as to why I held Jesus in such high esteem, then he listened to me patiently explain my personal spiritual views.

Tanoshi looked inscrutable, then pensive, and answered: "Mmm."

I think this utterance must be a complete sentence in Japanese, like the word "dude" is when it's used in California.

Tanoshi's visit coincided with Chris' return from college for the summer. Since Chris was old enough to be more like a pal to his dad than a responsibility, it was agreed upon that he'd spend the summer at his dad's house, where the rules weren't well-defined or enforced.

He would be living with his sister, Lauren, who had defected to her dad's residence a few months before when she heard the news of his new wife's pregnancy. Our daughter was fearful the new baby would replace her entirely.

My ever-helpful teens introduced the twenty-one-year-old, but still innocent, Tanoshi to the bar drinking game, Quarters. After curfew one late evening, they dropped Tanoshi's sodden body onto my couch.

"I drunk." Tanoshi giggled and slid like a snake from his seated position to become a puddle on the floor.

My delinquents fled, belly laughing with glee.

Rick put a pillow under Tanoshi's head and threw a blanket over him. "That's our boy!" he said and headed off for bed.

Near the end of our time with one another, I asked Tanoshi what he planned to do with his future, hoping the experience in the United States assisted with his process.

"Same plan. I kill self when thirty."

"What?" I clutched at my chest, hoping I misunderstood.

"Kill self at thirty. In Japan, I must do what society say. Get good job for money. I cannot survive this hell. Must be writer or die. No plobrem."

Stopping for coffee, I struggled for wisdom. I tried to explain that in America, a person can do or become whatever they choose and suggested he move here permanently and avoid a premature death.

His brow furrowed as he contemplated the rebellious suggestion. "Maybe I can act like Amelican and stay in Japan." Tanoshi said. He stressed that he must be very brave to become a writer in a society that disapproved of him making such a choice.

I mentally translated his serious declaration. Tanoshi's mixture of "r's" and "l's" was now familiar, even charming to my ears.

"Rick and I agree with your choice. You would break my heart if you killed yourself. You have a great gift for telling stories and are unique for your ability to think outside the box. Please, please give your writing a try…for me!"

Unbidden, the Voice, silent for a few years, clearly said, "Nice missionary work with Tanoshi! You've got a good start on your duty tour with the Japanese."

I tucked away the Voice's comment since it didn't make much sense to me at the time. Later, I'd recall it in a quite different situation.

The following year, Tanoshi's parents and aunt surprised us by asking to tour Yellowstone with Rick and me. With great effort, I coerced my parents to attend a small welcoming dinner at a nearby Japanese restaurant in honor of Tanoshi's relatives.

My father jokingly suggested he wear his military uniform and bring his sword. My mom just kept making disturbing noises under her breath.

The gentle Japanese contingent brought a cornucopia of gifts for everyone in the family, and it appeared to be a one-sided Christmas celebration instead of a simple dinner.

My parents gradually warmed to their generosity and their honest outpouring of love for Rick and me. With inventive hand gestures, and despite a few misunderstandings via the language barriers, the evening proved a stupendous success.

In two short hours, we erased decades of fear and hatred caused by governments, not ordinary people.

Rick and I accepted the honor of appearing as the best man and maid of honor at the extravagant wedding of Tanoshi and his bride, Kireina. The event occurred just after Tanoshi's almost fatal thirtieth birthday. At the reception, Tanoshi came to sit by me and to thank me for making a positive difference in his life.

I said, "I am glad you did not kill yourself."

He replied with a smile, "Me, too."

Tanoshi's new wife joined us, put her hand on my shoulder, and added sincerely, "Me, too!"

57

Earthquake

In October of 1989, Rick and I planned to visit Tanoshi and his family in Japan.

Although Rick struggled with leaving his factory in the charge of others for ten days, he reluctantly promised to accompany me for an overdue vacation.

Two days prior to our departure, a 7.1 earthquake destroyed our town and killed seven people. To describe the situation as chaotic and overwhelmingly horrifying is a serious understatement.

A massive number of people faced despair in a nature-made hell and received eternal post-traumatic stress as a free bonus. I was one of them.

Seconds before the event, I sat quietly at my desk in the office I shared with three others, who were currently out and about. I faced a huge plate glass window that looked out onto a street one block from the business district.

Without warning, my desk began to rock back and forth. A vase of flowers from Rick toppled to the floor, shattering glass in every direction. A large wooden sign suspended on chains in the front window began to twist to and fro, striking the window in rhythm with the rocking of the furniture.

Instinctively, I sought shelter beneath my desk, knocking my chair over as I scrambled woozily on the shifting floor. My head banged repeatedly against the wooden insides of my former chair space.

As the seemingly endless assault escalated and continued, I peeked out to observe our bank of five-drawer file cabinets hop and dance across the floor like advancing chorus girls.

I'm going to die, I thought. *I wonder if Rick will survive?*

Gradually, the shaking ceased, and I froze under my desk, taking stock of my situation. Thanking God that the picture window was spared, I crawled from beneath the desk and ventured to the glass front door.

I looked across the street at what could have been a scene in a disaster movie. Screaming people ran in all directions. One man sat atop his car, covering his face with shaking hands. A short, jarring aftershock caused me to swear like a sailor.

Lifting my gaze to the commercial buildings, I noticed a cloud of dust from ruined concrete rise like smoke.

Car alarms blared from all directions, and an explosive blast from somewhere down the block attracted the sirens of several fire trucks.

My head felt muddled from shock and the battering under my desk. I went into survival mode as I found my purse and fished out my car keys. As if in slow motion, I walked to the front door and locked it, avoiding another glimpse at the panic on the other side of the cracked door glass.

Deliberately, I circled the cabinets in the middle of the room and the multitude of office paraphernalia strewn all over the floor, as if the situation were perfectly normal.

Opening the rear door that led to our reserved parking, my ears were re-assaulted by a cacophony of unsettling sounds. I endeavored to block them out by singing a nonsensical lullaby as loudly as my constricted throat could manage. This gave me something to do other than join my voice with the others who were going berserk.

Fearing an outbreak of vandalism, or having my car usurped, I locked the rear office door, entered my vehicle, and proceeded cautiously from the parking lot. Slowing for the people wandering aimlessly and slamming on my brakes for those darting in front of the car, I tried to concentrate on my breathing.

"I must get home" was my mantra. I couldn't allow any other thought to enter my brain and cause me to overload and shut down.

Somehow, I managed to reach the freeway and work my way into the solid stretch of vehicles imperceptibly moving in either direction. Drivers seemed exceptionally polite, allowing people to enter the convoy ahead of them. I guessed we were experiencing group shock.

Forty minutes later, halfway through my two-mile drive, I noticed something potentially suicidal happening as we crept toward the overpass.

As a vehicle crested the rise, an apparent shift in one of the connecting concrete panels caused a gap of approximately six inches to the formally adjoining panel.

Each approaching driver was required to speed up to get their car or truck fully across the divide or risk hanging up halfway, thus stopping all traffic indefinitely.

Watching the process, and knowing I had no choice but to duplicate it, I inched forward in a state of high anxiety. It was abundantly clear that sooner or later an unlucky car or truck would be the metaphorical straw to break the overpass' back and plunge to destruction and death.

Will it be me?

As my turn to cross arrived, I removed my foot from the brake, transferred it to the gas pedal, pushed hard, and prayed.

58

Home Sweet Home

I finally arrived home to assess the damage and find safety. There was an abundance of the former and none of the latter.

The earthquake occurred on a cold fall day in the late afternoon, and the daylight was disappearing. I flipped a useless light switch and soon realized the whole area had lost electrical power.

My first order of business was to locate candles and matches. Accomplishing that feat, I tried to call Rick at work, but the telephone line was dead.

In the dim house, I noted my open kitchen cabinet doors indicated a lack of contents, and my eyes widened at the collection of mixed glass blanketing the tile floor. There were kitchen appliances, mixing bowls, and pots and pans added for effect.

Rick's treasured collection of orchids, formerly showcased on our fireplace mantel, was now dumped unceremoniously on the beige carpet.

Beside the horticultural graveyard lay our new television set, face down.

Amid continuing aftershocks, I grabbed a broom and swept the kitchen-floor glass into a corner. Next, I reached into the refrigerator and grabbed cheese, apples, and a recently opened bottle of wine.

After retrieving a plastic cup from the rubble, I located our battery-operated radio, snatched a small blanket from the couch, and hurried to the front porch. A strong aftershock prompted me to scream as I wobbled.

I closed the door behind me to retain the heat, dropped into a patio chair, waved hello to my neighbors in the cul-de-sac who were doing the same thing, and proceeded to gulp my wine.

Aftershocks of varying strengths and durations continued, each one causing a return to hellishly fearful anxiety.

As the blessed balm of chardonnay proceeded to take the edge off my shattered nerves, my thoughts turned to Rick.

This murderous earthquake not only destroyed lives and property, but its tragic repercussions would also include an unalterable rift in Rick's and my relationship.

59

No Do-Over Available

After the earthquake, many of the telephone landlines functioned badly, or not at all. The first call I received, several hours after the event, was from Tanoshi in Japan. He told me our earthquake was front-page news worldwide.

His concerns included our wellbeing and if we were still planning to visit in two days. Although pleased to hear from him, I could not honestly answer either question and promised to call him back after I contacted Rick.

Suddenly, I remembered Rick saying he would be taking his car in for service that morning and he'd be retrieving it in the late afternoon. I had assumed he had been at the factory when the earthquake occurred.

By midnight, only my grandmother, Opal, had gotten through, but I had no word from Rick. My parents were on a tour of the Holy Land and in a different time zone. I had no idea if they could contact us.

I attempted to call Rick's factory but was met with busy signals until my eighth try. I realized there could be tragic consequences in the huge facility with its two hundred employees. Rick's second in command, Mitch, breathlessly answered the phone, and I had to shout to make him hear me over the background noise.

"Is Rick OK?" I screamed.

"What? Rick OK? Yah, he's awful busy right now. I'll tell him you called."

Before Mitch could hang up on me, I shouted, "No, I'll wait on the line while you find him."

Many long minutes later, Rick's stressed voice began a monologue, "It's a mess here, Rach. Nobody was killed, but I've had injuries, and the machinery is damaged. Don't expect me home anytime soon."

Rick sounded like he was about to end the alleged conversation, so I quickly raised my voice and said, "Hey, honey, I'm alright. Gosh, don't worry about me." It came out just as sarcastically as I meant it to.

He picked up the insinuation and defended himself, "I was at the car dealership when the quake hit. I jumped into the car and drove right by your office. It was still standing, so I presumed you were OK. Then I hurried to the factory to take care of things here. It's my responsibility, for heaven's sake."

Did he feel those nails pounding into the coffin of our relationship like I did?

"I guess you won't be going to Japan like you promised," I ventured.

Rick said, "You go. It'll be good for you to get out of here for ten days and let things settle down."

I heard, "My job is more important than you are, and that's a fact of life."

Although I traveled to Japan and enjoyed the pampering of Tanoshi's kind family, my feelings were irreparably hurt by Rick's choices.

I loved Rick with all my heart and fought to recall all the years of my feeling happy, content, and valued by him. His kindness and generosity with my children proved him a better father than their biological one.

However, I wondered how long I could hold out before I sought affection and fun with someone else. Technically we were engaged, but it was more than obvious that Rick was married to his job, and loneliness ate at my soul.

Our relationship limped along for many more months, but Rick didn't seem to perceive the change.

60

The Bad News

One evening, Rick excitedly shared the good news of his probable promotion to upper management. He glossed over the part where he'd be transferred to the East Coast and added under his breath that his extra responsibilities would demand the need for his full time and attention.

Instead of sharing his happiness, my spirits sank.

Although Rick assured me we could continue a successful (in his mind) relationship, my earlier memories of being repeatedly uprooted began to haunt me.

The security and fulfillment generated by my successful business, and the proximity to my family and friends, provided a support system irreplaceable by a lonely life in an ivory tower back East.

Rick's relocation for the promotion wasn't imminent, but it served as the catalyst for prompting us to gradually, and painfully, disentangle our lives.

We never separated our hearts.

61

Broccoli Battle

Eventually, I told Rick of my plan to move to an apartment for six months to take the opportunity to consider whether or not to continue our engagement.

Although he expressed shock and dismay at our temporary parting, he agreed to give me some space.

At first, we continued our Friday dinners, but gradually Rick excused himself, citing long hours at work. His upcoming transfer to New York forced employee shifting and intensive training in the upper management positions. A perfectionist, Rick monitored everything.

One evening, Rick telephoned to inform me that his father's doctor gave Herbert a life expectancy of three months due to an aggressive lung cancer diagnosis.

The last time I had visited Rick's folks for a family dinner, Herbert and I danced around a potentially dangerous exchange with great success. It involved broccoli.

With the usual suspects circling the informal dining table, we enjoyed a simple meal of fried chicken, baked potatoes, salad, and broccoli. A two-tiered fudge chocolate cake, Beth's specialty, lay temptingly on the kitchen counter and was the focus of the young nephew's longing gaze.

Marcus fidgeted as he awaited the grownups' final bites, and this caught Herbert's attention. "No dessert for you, young man," said Grandpa Herbert. "Got to finish your broccoli first."

The lad's face fell, and he glanced at his mother for a doubtful reprieve, but she knew not to defy Herbert's orders.

Emboldened by Herbert's and my budding friendship, I raised my voice, "Guess Grandpa Herbert doesn't get any cake either. He didn't eat any broccoli."

The old saying "you could have heard a pin drop" popped into my mind as I glanced at the horrified faces of the adults staring in my direction.

"What did you say?" queried my almost father-in-law with a challenge in his rising voice.

"I said, Grandpa needs to set a good example and take a bite of broccoli before he gets any dessert."

No one breathed as they glanced between Herbert's and my stubborn gazes. I must admit my heart was pounding as I felt Rick squeeze my hand under the table in an effort to reign me in.

The wall clock ticked eight seconds off loudly as Herbert's wheels turned, then he slowly and deliberately used his fork to spear a small portion of broccoli from the serving dish and placed it into his opened mouth with a flourish.

My peripheral vision noted Marcus mimic the action, flourish and all.

As the battle raged between the alpha adults' locked eyes, both of the males chewed and swallowed.

"Well," I chirped and glanced triumphantly around the table, "looks like everybody gets dessert."

Later, Rick confessed to me that our broccoli duel was the only time a family member ever stood up to his father.

There would be one final time.

62

Herbert's Friend

Rick unhappily accepted my temporary transition to a new life as permanent. However, as Herbert's time ran out, Rick begged a favor of me. He explained that this final, intensely emotional visit with his father required my comforting presence.

I couldn't say no.

Rick's invitation supplied me a chance to say goodbye to Herbert as well, and my heart ached at the thought of it. I had been praying faithfully every morning for Herbert to experience a peaceful death.

Hebert professed to be a lifelong atheist.

The brothers had purchased a comfortable recliner for their ailing father at Christmas. Herbert's weight had declined alarmingly, and he looked like a child in its sturdy cushions.

All of Beth and Herbert's children gathered in the living room around the recliner. Voices were hushed and the tone somber.

Beth hovered over Herbert with a small glass of orange juice, declaring in a loving manner that the doctor said he was to keep hydrated. Herbert swiped at the offending glass, growled he didn't want it, and ordered her to leave him alone.

As I hovered in the background, unsure of what to say or do, Beth sought me out and handed me the glass. She said, "He'll drink it for you. Please, Rach, he needs the liquid."

With all eyes on me, I approached the sad throne and offered the juice to Herbert. "I don't want it!" he barked, then proceeded to cough violently.

I leaned in after he caught his ragged breath and whispered, "You need to drink the damned orange juice so Beth feels better. Chug it right now, or I'll pour it over your head!"

He jolted upright and gaped at me. "By God, you'd do it!" he said. "Give me that fool thing." He drank it down in three gulps, handed me back the glass, and said with a lilting voice, "Are you happy now?"

As I leaned in to kiss his stubbled face, he grabbed my hand and hissed, "You have to promise me to take care of my boy, Rachael. It's a dying man's wish; you must promise me."

I stuttered that Rick and I were no longer engaged, and I couldn't promise. His grip tightened, and he repeated the request between debilitating coughs.

When I finally agreed, Herbert looked straight into my soul and saw my honest acceptance. How could I know the promise I gave that day, and one I ultimately kept, would be at my own deadly peril?

After the funeral, we all gathered at Beth's home. My daughter, Lauren, attended with me and we handed each other Kleenex during the service. Many people I had never met attended, and I even chatted with Rick's former wife.

As Lauren and I prepared to leave, Beth took us each by the hand and asked us to accompany her to Herbert's room; the place he died.

In hushed tones, she pointed to the empty double bed and explained how wonderful hospice had been to them in his final weeks. She reminded us that Herbert never professed a belief in God and didn't attend church services with her except at Christmas.

I waited for the point of her story as she struggled to continue.

"Do you believe in angels?" she finally managed.

"Of course I do. Why?" I answered gently

"Well, Herbert was frightened to die and worried about it all the time."

"Recently, when I came in to bring his medications, Herbert told me he wasn't afraid to die anymore. He pointed to the foot of his bed and said his new friend sat there. Herbert explained he was a nice young man, although he dressed kind of funny, and was staying with him until he died. They would go home together."

"The next morning, I found that Herbert had passed in his sleep. He looked completely at ease. What do make of that?"

Lauren and I smiled at one another.

"I believe God sent him an angel and that Herbert's in heaven," I replied.

My daughter nodded her agreement, and the three of us shared a hug.

I felt the old scallywag join in.

63

Mexican Sunsets

Ernie and Connie Catch Dinner

Rick's and my relationship shifted only slightly over the following years. Discernible differences manifested as separate addresses and lack of physical intimacy, already diminished over the years due to his working late hours. We inevitably drifted apart.

Unfettered by my office-bound partner, I agreed to venture to Puerto Vallarta later in the year for a week of sun and Coronas with my newly divorced girlfriend, Connie. Neither of us, now in our mid-forties, ever before dared foreign travel unchaperoned by our husbands. This trip promised to baptize us into the world of independent, single, working mothers.

Ex-husbands were coerced into housing their children during our escape, and she and I made plans. We arranged leave from our jobs and attempted to soothe our parents' fears.

At the San Jose airport, we dubiously awaited the boarding of our Mexican airplane at a makeshift waiting area marked by a hand-drawn cardboard sign.

A half hour after the departure time marked upon our tickets, an ununiformed, middle-aged, Spanish-speaking woman gestured for us to follow her down a flight of stairs while we carried our own luggage.

This woman doubled, or rather, tripled, as cocktail hostess and ticket collector, as well as directed us, in Spanish, on and off the plane. God only knows what else her duties included.

My friend and I, befuddled at the casual boarding, overheard a group of party guys ask her where to store the chickens. Great hilarity erupted among the seasoned travelers as I considered flying the coop myself and returning to the safety of home.

With no rhyme or reason, the mostly middle-aged men shoved into seats and began ringing the overhead buttons for margaritas. A particularly obnoxious, boisterous gang of six caused us to sniff in disapproval.

Already filled to the gills with cerveza, they regaled the small plane's vacationers with tall tales of their fishing skills.

Being of delicate stomach, I required a window seat, but none remained after the onslaught of men took over the plane. Not to be deterred, I asked a fellow from the gang, now hogging a window, if he'd please trade my middle seat for his. A firm shaking of his head indicated my best option to be near a window meant sitting next to him.

I plunked down with irritation and announced loudly to my girlfriend in the aisle seat next to me, "Well, guess I'll just be barfing the whole way to Mexico. How long's the flight anyway?"

Like a jack-in-the-box, my reluctant neighbor hopped up and unceremoniously scrambled over our feet, gesturing for us to move over as he settled into the aisle seat.

After takeoff, he dozed off, causing his head to drift onto Connie's shoulder.

Connie, a private person, used two fingers to nudge his head upright, but he rebounded to nestle against Connie's ample bosom. A full-on shove of his face resulted in his listing to the opposite direction for the remainder of the flight.

Fate chuckled as Connie and I struggled with an abundance of luggage at the P.V. airport and finally located our bus to the hotel. Upon entering the vehicle, we shuddered to find the gang of six from the airplane the only other passengers in the cramped and dilapidated vehicle. They exchanged distressed glances and lost their party verve.

We ran into them everywhere and eventually gave up and joined them for beer and dancing at a popular cantina. Connie and I accepted their invitation for a day-long fishing trip on their leader's fishing yacht.

Connie caught a colorful dorado as I lay green with seasickness on the deck. Between unladylike bouts of vomiting, I weakly begged them to throw me overboard to die with the sharks.

Captain Ray regretted not dropping me to shore, he said later, as the men secured the boat at the dock. I had literally crawled down the gangplank, too weak to stand. Ray hollered at me to get up because I was making his boat look bad. I managed to wave him a one-fingered salute with my carefully manicured hand.

Ray sought to make it up to me with a meal out the following night. His offer to treat me to a fish dinner induced a fresh round of gags.

After our late make-up dinner, Ray walked me home, and as we stared at the early morning starlit sky from my deck, he shared the upheaval caused by his recent divorce. We commiserated as I shared my rift with Rick, and we toasted our long-neck bottles, warming to each other.

Over two years of infrequent get-togethers, Ray and I eventually enjoyed a crazy, fun-filled relationship together in a small fishing community in northern California. Ray encouraged my adventurous side, and I reveled in the freedom to express this facet of myself for the first time.

My parents disapproved of Ray's invitation to accompany him to retrieve his boat at the tip of Baja, Mexico one spring. The three-week trek promised dust and danger, an opportunity I couldn't resist, and the journey exceeded my expectations.

Ray, a 6'4" hulk of a hunter and fisherman, was in his early forties and qualified as a bodyguard in my book. His gentle demeanor masked a capable ability to take care of almost any challenging situation with a minimum of effort.

After Ray's coaching on the way to the border, I learned of tactics required in upcoming possibly dangerous situations. One brush with a fair-sized contingent of armed and testy Federales found me provocatively leaping from the truck. Heads turned and smiles appeared as I waved my map and sang out, "Por favor, señor?"

As a ribboned, uniformed young man with a machine gun slung over one shoulder came to my rescue, I engaged him in an attempt to find the way to our next town using hand signals and giggles.

My travel partner had barked this instruction quickly as we were waved over at a barbed-wire barrier. Ray hoped this attempt at distraction from the boat repair equipment in the back of our large vehicle might prevent confiscation.

As the flustered soldier gaped from me in shorts and a midriff-baring top to the map, his superior officer admonished him in rapid Spanish and pointed for me to return to the truck. The armed and potentially dangerous stranger then slid neatly in beside me.

With my companion busy with other officials in the rear of the vehicle, my officer nodded for my approval as he opened our glove compartment. He smiled broadly, exposing unfortunate teeth, as he discovered my legal stash of chewing gum.

"Ah," he said, as he fished out all of the packages, "I like. Gracias, señorita."

I startled the officer and caused my companion to race to the front seat when I grabbed at the chewing gum and replied, "No!"

"Nooooo?" said the officer, unused to such a reaction.

"*No?*" croaked my disapproving and uneasy companion.

"Por favor, señor," I pleaded as I put my fisted hands up and imitated driving the car, then started bouncing up and down, mimicking the ruts in the Mexican road. Next, I grabbed my stomach and made gagging sounds.

I drew a crowd but continued my pantomime.

I took a stick of gum, unwrapped it, and began chewing furiously, patting my stomach. Then I turned and gave the confused, pistol-carrying man a big smile as I held up my hands in victory.

Thank God, my boyfriend pulled a pair of cold Coca Colas from our cooler and offered them both to the baffled officer. This, Ray figured, might distract him from using his trigger finger.

After a shake of his head in the affirmative to let me know he understood, Señor Federale retreated calmly from my side to leave the loca gringa to go about her way with her chewing gum.

The gate parted as we rolled forward, but we remained wary of any last-minute change of mind from the army.

“Are you nuts?” boomed my quivering protector as he checked the rear-view mirror and picked up speed.

Although Ray remained speechless for many miles after the incident, I heard Grandma Rachael’s uproarious laughter in my head. It was the trip of a lifetime, and I loved every minute of it.

Ray and I often spent time with his best friend, Ernie. Their friendship went back decades, and Ernie taught Ray everything he knew about fishing and boating, which amounted to more than most folks ever knew.

Although Ernie was a man’s man, his multifaceted charm and charisma extended to the ladies, too. He reminded me of Dean Martin, my mom’s favorite entertainer, with thick, wavy grey hair and a captivating sly smile. His robin-egg blue eyes sparkled with good humor, and his quick wit leaned to clever but not biting.

Ernie charmed me, too, and we enjoyed a warm friendship devoid of lust.

Ray and I frequently stayed over at Ernie's upscale modern home when traveling and enjoyed his homemade gourmet meals every time. We played dominoes and drank beer, dreaming of our next trip to Mexico together.

On an Easter Sunday, when Ernie and his steady lady, Gwen, stayed at our home up north, I coerced everyone to join me at Mass for the occasion. Under duress, they humored me, but Ernie warned me of a probable lighting strike to the church because he claimed that God didn't love him.

Ernie received no formal religious upbringing but was the nicest person I ever met.

I countered his warning with, "Ernie, everybody in this car loves you. How could God not love you?" He looked thoughtful, and the conversation ended on that note.

Ernie shared his love of gardening with me and his future plans for transforming his weedy adjacent lot into a garden of Eden. The last time we stayed with Ernie, the spacious cleared lot sported a cornucopia of potting containers filled with roses, hedges and perennials, an unassembled arbor and bench, and boxes of flower seeds.

As Ernie spread his arms wide, he regaled me with ambitious plans for a wonderland he expected to produce by the following spring. I promised to return for a personal tour, even though I knew Ray and I planned to part ways in the next few months.

After five years of good news concerning his prostate cancer treatment, Ernie looked forward to his official "all clear" from his physician the following Monday. Over our final meal together, I wished him good luck on his prognosis and hugged Ernie goodbye.

I never saw Ernie in his earthly garden, but a year later, I saw him in a better one.

64

Rick's Undoing

Shortly before leaving for his new assignment in New York, Rick noticed a large lump in his neck while shaving. He finagled a drop-in visit with his doctor, who insisted he take a few necessary tests. Rick stalled, citing the upcoming relocation, but promised to attend to the matter when he settled in after his move.

By the time Rick consulted a new doctor, the consensus was leukemia. He required immediate treatment at a research hospital. After several consultations at three research facilities, Rick planned to seek admission to an advanced program in Washington State.

Rick had recently met a lovely lady in his apartment complex, and they dated for a few months. Since the research hospital required two full-time caregivers for him in order to qualify for their program, she agreed to participate, but only as his wife, and he reluctantly became engaged.

Moving on to the task of acquiring his second caregiver, Rick planned to phone me but struggled with how to drop the bomb.

65

Solemn Visit

Since neither Ray nor I desired another marriage, we enjoyed our relationship with no strings attached, retaining the ability to exit without complications. We stayed together several years for the sheer fun of it.

One night, Rick phoned from the East Coast and asked to come visit me, saying it was important.

The evening Rick arrived, he joined Ray and me for dinner at a popular restaurant in our town. The conversation seemed trivial, and I noted that Rick's appearance had changed. His skin, dull and unusually pale, pulled tight across his cheekbones.

When Ray excused himself to visit the restroom, I asked Rick point-blank, "OK, what's going on? This is not like you."

He pulled no punches. "I have leukemia, Rach."

My mouth agape and tears forming quickly in my widened eyes, he continued softly.

"I need your help."

Ray returned to the table and halted when he observed the scene. "This can't be good," he muttered.

After our meeting, and the news Rick imparted, I bade a reluctant goodbye to Ray.

My footloose and fancy-free lifestyle was about to change dramatically.

66

The Call

While staying with my daughter after moving out of Ray's and my home, I spent a lot of time in prayer, asking God for guidance. After several weeks of indecision, I had the following experience and wrote it as an essay. In retrospect, it was a prophecy.

MISSIONARY? *12/4/98*

I had a great "talk" with God this morning after Mass. It was First Friday, with Adoration of the Eucharist, so I stayed to chat a bit and thank Him for everything in my life.

My mind wandered into a detailed reverie featuring how nice it'd be to remain in Colorado with my daughter's family, join the St. Luke's Singles Club, find a Christian husband, work full-time at the Greater Europe Mission, and...

A Voice, sounding like God speaking, broke into my thoughts with, "NO, I need you to continue being a missionary."

"Excuse me?" I said to the curious Voice in my head. "A what?"

God caused me to recall I've been "bait for the Lord," as I call myself, most of my life.

He ran a video in my mind of my first boyfriend telling me how he had read the Bible from front to back, on a dare from me, and became a Christian. Next came my first husband's conversion, and then my ex-fiancé's baptism.

God reminded me of the names of numerous friends who attended church with me, of my answering their questions about God, His unconditional love and forgiveness.

"Oh, yes," I said, as I recalled the many opportunities to serve.

The Voice continued with how He arranged for me to work at the Greater Europe Mission so that I might understand how important it is for missionaries to experience an occasional "R and R."

When they begin to burn out, He reminds them of their purpose, and a heavenly reward. The respite, like this time for me in Colorado with my daughter, is necessary, but missionaries belong in the trenches.

A missionary's job isn't found in the safety and comfort of a practicing congregation. The blessing of numerous previous communities provided me support, but static involvement with them is not my life's mission.

So, I agree to step back into the fray. Helping where I can and being "loving, kind, and generous," constantly praying to be improved so that I can do good in spite of who I currently am.

I am forever amazed when God picks us weak and sinful people to reach out and bring

His love. With perfect servants, His wondrous works wouldn't be so obvious.

With depression's siren song inviting me to despair, following another heartbreak and failed relationship, I feel rescued again!

Thanks, God.

67

One Last Chance

Desiring my input on his future wife, Rick purchased an airline ticket for me to visit him on the East Coast. Angie, his new fiancée, seemed a complicated young woman, unhappy at her life's circumstances. Rick's wealth and success attracted many women. It didn't appear to be a good match, but I felt compelled to remain neutral.

Being a woman, I felt a twinge of jealousy, but it passed. Rick's health was of the utmost importance, and we needed two caregivers.

When Angie took a few days to visit her mother, Rick and I spent time reminiscing, voicing regrets, and discussing his future tribulations as a cancer patient.

After a tour of his new world in a beautiful company car, we returned to his penthouse apartment overlooking the huge harbor and lofty skyline. Rick took my hands and said, "It's always been you I hoped to marry, Rach. Do you think you could change your mind? I really need you."

Taking a very deep breath, my mind and soul communicated, and I answered with a question, "If we did marry, and you survived this ordeal, could you promise me to resign from this hectic lifestyle and find a way to spend more time together as a couple?"

The familiar gleam in his pale blue eyes and his soft smile prepared me for his answer. Always an honest man, he gave an honest answer, "Now, Rach, you know I can't promise you that."

In the Spring of 1999, my former fiancé, Rick, his bride, and I moved in together. Our furnished apartment, within walking distance of the hospital, provided two bedrooms and a single bathroom.

Angie and I enrolled in the required formal caregiver's class at the research hospital, admitted Rick into his program, and settled into a routine.

We organized, prepared, and readied ourselves to fight as a team for Rick's life. The estimated time required for all the procedures was from three to five months.

We enjoyed a little sightseeing and a beautiful spring in the Pacific Northwest with our remaining free time.

Month after month, we rejoiced as Rick's test results proved favorable and mourned when they took a turn for the worse. He was in and out of the hospital often, and both venues proved difficult for the three of us.

To keep Rick company when hospitalized, his wife and I took long shifts. This arrangement was erratic because of his numerous emergencies, and none of us got enough sleep.

When people asked how Rick managed to get two good-looking caregivers, he introduced us as his wife and girlfriend. To keep people on their toes, Angie and I took turns being introduced as his wife. This drove the nurses nuts.

The truth remained, Rick was accompanied by two women who loved him dearly and would do everything in their collective power to help him survive this terrible ordeal.

The situation complicated when Rick's wife took a tumble on some steps, breaking her foot. Angie no longer shared the unending list of chores: shopping, cooking, extensive cleaning, running to the hospital, and driving. She was on crutches for weeks, and the entirety of the day and night responsibilities fell to me.

Early one morning, as I carefully cleaned the area around Rick's chest tube, we sat in companionable silence. Only inches apart, we absentmindedly observed each other's appearances.

In the former days of our living together, and raising my family, we dressed in business attire and always appeared well groomed and businesslike in the daylight hours.

Now we wore rumpled bedclothes, fly-away hairdos, and sported dark bags under our eyes. We blended more with the homeless Seattleites than with our former peers.

Yet I felt honored, content, and joyful to be there.

With his abundant generosity and kindness to me and my family, I often felt I could never repay him. My current roles as his nurse, cook, and chauffeur served as a pittance compared to his countless gifts to us.

As I continued my ministrations with rubbing alcohol and Q-tips, I uncontrollably yawned. Rick looked deep into my eyes and smiled gently.

I recalled the words he asked me to remember as our relationship blossomed many years ago: *You will never need to tell me you love me. I will know by the way you treat me.*

68

Something Fun

After the first couple of months living in exceptionally close quarters, Rick's new bride suggested I take a night off each month and "do something fun." In addition, she inferred the honeymooners needed to enjoy a little privacy.

Music sounded enticing, dancing even better. For many years, my single friends and I had gone dancing several nights a week, and I missed those fun times. I perused a local entertainment magazine for ideas.

I attended a Parents Without Partners dance without success, other than to accept two one-time dinner dates, both resulting in marriage proposals.

The first man proposed our marriage over a pre-dinner drink, apologizing for the short notice as he spoke dispassionately of his need for a wife and children before he got too old.

I felt compelled to ask why he chose me for the honor, and he replied that I was a good dancer, pretty, and seemed easy to talk to.

After the shock of learning I was fifty-two, and a mother of two grown children, I accepted the compliment of his imagining me to be ten years younger than I was, and he called for the check.

My ex-date asked if we should split the cost of the fine wine, and I shook my head in the negative while bolting mine down. With no dinner forthcoming, we raced each other to the parking lot and parted ways in separate cars.

These were strange times. People in their late forties seemed to have delayed marriage and children in favor of higher education and careers. Now the biological clocks were clanging, and I sensed a grasping for babies I couldn't relate to.

A second date, with a gentleman from Australia, proved equally surprising. He asked me to meet him at a large, well-known restaurant. At the dance, he had mentioned how he entered the United States on a work visa, which would expire shortly.

As I now walked tentatively into a huge dining room, I noticed a lengthy reserved table with a dozen or more people standing around talking. There were several children in the group.

A man's voice at the table called out my name, and I was startled to find my date charging toward me. He excitedly called to the others, announcing my arrival. Sounds of approval and their exchanging of happy glances put me on high alert, and I retreated backward into the hall with my date hot on my trail.

"What's all this?" I queried. An old television show, entitled *This Is Your Life*, flashed through my mind. Each week, a guest was surprised with a bouquet of roses and a dais to sit upon as multitudes of family and friends spoke to the nation of the chosen one's life.

"Just a few of my family and friends wanting to meet my fiancée," he said in an attempt to calm my anxiety.

"Fiancée?" I croaked. "We don't even know each other's last names."

"Mine is Hopper." He smiled. "And yours?"

As I fled to the exit door in high heels, he caught up with me and grabbed my arm.

"Listen," he pleaded. "I told you at the dance that I've been in the country working as a carpenter and wanted to live here permanently, and you seemed to encourage me to do so. My visa is expiring, and all I'm asking is for you to marry me for a few months. Then we can get divorced, and I can stay here. No big deal, right, mate?"

"Sorry, mate!" I answered. Waving goodbye to the surprised family and friends, I left the party early.

Two months dragged by, and I was tempted to attend a monthly Seattle Yacht Club Singles dance at a nearby restaurant. Rick and Angie had pleaded with me to get out for a break after some tough weeks of disappointing test results.

I phoned my mom, who was fully aware that I became deathly seasick on any vessel, and shared my plan to mingle with a boating group. She suggested sarcastically that I join a single's parachuting group while at it. My fear of heights was also well documented.

I put the dance date on our commune calendar and fussed over what I would wear. Later, as I entered a large room full of people I didn't know, my "new kid" complex kicked in. Fighting the urge to reverse direction and flee, I took a deep breath and looked for a seat at a table.

It was soon apparent most of the members had renewed their memberships over many years and secured the choice tables with fixed seating arrangements.

I noticed a roomy round table in a corner with eight empty chairs and formulated a plan. After claiming my prize by draping my wrap and purse over one chair, I watched as new people entered the door, and began checking their expressions.

Many of the entrants walked confidently inside, waved at compatriots, and strode immediately to reserved seats.

Then, a woman my age entered, looked around frantically while clutching her purse to her chest, and crept in. As she neared my table, I called out, "Are you new, too? Wanna sit with me?"

In the blink of an eye, a smile lit her face and she claimed a chair. We chatted as I shared my plan, and together we scanned for more newcomers. Within fifteen minutes, we snagged five more unattached ladies of varying ages.

The band was warming up, and we had one spot left.

A very handsome and nicely dressed younger man wandered by. He reminded me of my shy son and decided he could be my next target. As he turned to scout the room, I noticed he was wearing a short-sleeved shirt and his left arm had been amputated just before the elbow.

How courageous, I thought and called out, "Hey, we need a little male energy over here. Care to join us?"

Startled, the man turned and was greeted with seven smiling female faces. He laughed at our invitation, but plopped into the remaining chair. We introduced ourselves and happily awaited the music together.

It was a delightful evening.

As men swarmed to our table to meet fresh dance partners, one man grumbled aloud, "Why does this guy get to sit with seven lovely ladies and we have to cross this big floor to ask for a dance?"

"Because we are no fools," I answered. "We grabbed him first." Our male friend beamed but didn't seem anxious to dance.

"A good-looking fellow like you should get out there and let the ladies fight over you," I said. He looked down and shifted his shoulder so his left arm was facing me.

I grabbed his right hand and pulled him to the dance floor. He smiled and quickly picked up the pulsing beat. The floor was crowded, and

I noticed several young ladies dancing his way. As the song ended, one cheerfully said "Hello" to him as she moved closer.

Returning to my empty table, I smiled and waved at my former tablemates as they laughed and danced.

An hour later, as I slowly danced with a nice man, I spotted my former male tablemate dancing closely with the cheerful lady. When he noticed me, he mouthed, "Thank you!" and grinned.

What a great night!

69

A Friend In Need

Rick, Me, and Glen

The following month, I happily anticipated returning to the singles dance, and this time a single lady near the back of the room offered me a seat at her small table. After back-to-back dances with various partners, I returned to the table to sip my drink and rest while the band took a break.

I felt eyes on me from my right side and glanced over. A short fellow in strange attire smiled my way. The Yacht Club affair was a tad upscale, but this man wore long wrinkled shorts, a casual tee shirt, and dirty sneakers with white socks. This look worked as beach party attire but was not typically appropriate for a Yacht Club Singles gathering in downtown Seattle.

I wondered if he was lost, or worse, and jumped when he suddenly leaned over and asked, “Care to dance?”

I pointed to the empty band area and said slowly, as if to a deranged person, “There is no music right now.”

He countered, speaking just as slowly, “I know that, but every time I start over to ask you to dance, someone gets to you first. I just wanted to ask you now for when the music starts up again.”

The man remained standing next to my chair as if guarding me and became mute.

Maybe it’s time to go home, I thought.

I pointed to the door at the end of the room that led to a large balcony facing the water, then stood, excused myself, and muttered about needing some air.

“I’ll meet you right here when the band starts up,” I lied and headed for the balcony.

From prior experience, I knew the balcony contained a door at the other end leading back into the main room. My plan was to mosey to the balcony, escape into the crowd I knew would be there, work my way to the other door, exit the property, and disappear.

My plan worked up to the point where I began to exit the balcony. Standing in the middle of the doorway was the strange man who asked sweetly, "Are you trying to ditch me?"

Gotcha....

His name was Glen.

I felt better talking to Glen in the crowded space but began to shiver in the cold night air. Glen, attired in summer clothing, chatted about himself and questioned me.

Thankfully, the band started up before I turned blue, and he escorted me into the dance area.

As we danced and chatted, I actually began to have a good time. The similarities of our lives were amazing. We were both recently from California, and I found myself explaining why I was in Seattle. He listened thoughtfully.

When the evening drew to a close, Glen walked me to the restaurant's front door and asked if I wanted to go to Denny's for a cup of hot tea. Most guys in this situation offer to take me out for a "night cap" with a leer kicker.

As we sat at a small restaurant table, Glen held his hand out to me so we could say a prayer over our shared cheesecake and decaffeinated tea. He added a prayer for Rick, and I was touched.

Over the next few months, Glen occasionally shared dinners with Rick, Angie, and me at our apartment. He flew us to the San Juan Islands in his small airplane one sunny afternoon. The day was full of laughter and gave Rick a chance to feel “normal.” Our original trio had morphed into a quartet.

Since Glen lived about an hour away and held a full-time job, our dates were limited, but he phoned often. Glen and I weren’t ready for a long-term commitment but agreed to enjoy the present.

70

Strange Request

One Sunday morning, when the four of us awaited the commencement of Mass at the Catholic cathedral, a statue of Jesus pointing to His Sacred Heart caught my eye.

In my mind, the Voice, still active after many years, spoke to me clearly, “I need you to become a Lutheran.”

Since the time I first experienced the Voice, I tested any of its messages by asking myself honestly if this missive could possibly be my idea masquerading as Divine Intervention.

Indubitably, this request wasn’t the case.

Glen and his family, staunch Lutherans, often invited me to their services, but I knew from my Catholic upbringing that my attendance was not allowed except under extremely strict circumstances.

The Voice wasn’t requesting I attend a single service in the Protestant church but actually that I BECOME a Lutheran.

I closed my eyes, said an Our Father, and opened my eyes to stare at the stone statue again.

The message in my head repeated, this time with more emphasis.

I requested further information, as in "Really, why?" and "For how long?"

The Voice patiently and quickly replied, "Because I asked you to" and "I'll let you know later."

I reminded the Voice that my parents would not approve, although my boyfriend would be thrilled, and said this was the weirdest thing I had ever experienced.

The Mass started as the last of the message began echoing in my head, "Trust Me! Trust Me!"

Glen gladly brought me to his family's church service the following Sunday and introduced me to Pastor Russell. He welcomed me with open arms and invited Glen and me to join the choir. We sang for our fellow Lutherans at the noon service the following Sunday.

After two years as a Lutheran, I received an unexpected Voice message when Pastor Russell retired and a young bible-thumper, spouting fire and brimstone, took his place. It said, "You can go back to being a Catholic now."

Since Glen and I were missing Pastor Russell's uplifting sermons and loving hugs each Sunday anyway, I immediately defected to the local Catholic Church.

A few weeks later, Glen joined me, and we began attending Mass together.

71

A Great Loss

Many months passed as Rick, Angie, and I observed the medical test result numbers inch up (good) and then slide down (bad). Our spirits roller-coastered as hope prepared to leave the building.

Rick endured dialysis for several days when his kidneys threatened to quit. He was so miserable he begged us to let him die, but selfishly we encouraged him to endure.

When he developed a massive sinus infection, the thick pus drained down his throat, causing painful coughing spells. Rick insisted Angie or I sit with him around the clock to be available should he choke.

We ragged caregivers took shifts and passed each other between the apartment and the hospital at all hours of the day and night for almost a week. We blended in with the homeless and other night creatures, and our smell of death and near despair formed protective shields around us.

The second time Rick's sinus infection appeared, a week after the first cleared up, the left side of his face ballooned up and forced his eyelid closed. The skin of his cheek turned varying shades of green and blue.

Eventually, Rick lost all of his hair and his skin became mottled with purple bruises. Throughout all these trials and tribulations, Rick never lost his sense of humor or his courage. It broke my heart to see him in such misery.

The doctors finally reported that the cutting-edge procedures proved useless, and Rick's participation in research programs didn't pan out. He was thanked for his time and trouble, and we were told that maybe someone in the future would benefit from his efforts.

Our little team of three was exhausted and depleted. Rick was the first to give up, his wife followed, but I never did. Even after Rick attempted to say goodbye to me, I retorted, "You aren't going anywhere. You're slated to give my eulogy."

He just shook his head, gave me his loving smile, and said, "Now, Rach."

Rick's wife suggested that I find another place to live so she and her dying husband could have their final days together.

I would not leave the area as long as Rick survived, so I found an apartment about two hours from Seattle and procured a full-time job via an employment agency to pay for it. I had trouble sleeping and felt useless at my place of employment.

Glen lived an hour from me and an hour from Seattle, but we visited Rick every weekend, usually on both days.

Since Rick's immune system was virtually non-existent, we were forbidden to touch him in those final days because he could have transmitted troublesome germs to us.

The only physical contact allowable was to gently rub his hand as it lay covered by a stiff, white sheet.

When I found a spare minute, I cried.

Rick passed away a week before his fifty-fourth birthday. I learned of the event via his wife's phone call to my apartment. Thank God Glen was there to hold me as I started a long grieving process.

With Rick's demise, my fragile world slowly unraveled.

72

Unhappy New Year

Our former plans for ushering in the New Year with Rick were dashed, so we all decided to go our separate ways after the holidays concluded.

Giving a thirty-day notice to my apartment manager forced me to consider where I would be moving in 2000. My choices seemed few, and none of them appealing. I hated my current job but had nothing lined up anywhere else. Homeless, jobless, and broken-hearted, I prayed, not expecting much aid.

Pondering this looming dilemma, I sat in my uncomfortable rented chair and glanced over at the only book I read during the long sojourn in Seattle, *Still Me* by Christopher Reeve. I didn't have any idea what possessed me to purchase that rather depressing book.

Even though I had tossed it mercilessly in the trash twice, only to retrieve it later, I continued to drag myself through it for some unknown reason.

In the meantime, I endured a thankless Thanksgiving dinner with Glen's family.

The Christmas ritual proved more complicated since Angie needed to remain in

Seattle to finalize matters, and we naturally included her in many of the plans.

Glen invited me to his Annual Christmas Choir Concert in southern California. The two of us journeyed there in mid-December and stayed with his friends. A wonderful tenor, Glen had been a member of this celebrated ensemble for a couple of decades.

When Rick still had some energy, the four of us had planned to attend Christmas Eve Mass in the Cathedral, where for many months we stormed the heavens with our prayers. Now, the three of us would attend in his honor.

The final festivities included me, Angie, Glen, and a large number of Glen's family members. We were to spend a long New Year's weekend at a lodge in Oregon. Glen's encouragement to do something positive for the New Year helped make my decision to attend one final event together before Angie returned to the East Coast. The holiday schedule was set.

73

Best-Laid Plans

Things began badly when Glen's concert was sabotaged by a virulent influenza. Many of the choir members, including their conductor, either couldn't perform at all or wobbled on the platform, full of flu medication and in agony.

Following the grim performance, Glen insisted we dine with the conductor and his wife, both long-time friends of his. They coughed and shivered through the endless dinner, and I feared possible contagion at the extended hugs at our goodbyes.

Although I was required to be inoculated for flu and pneumonia prior to commencing my caregiver duties with Rick, my immune system had been pushed to its limits in the previous stressful, sleep-deprived months.

I developed painful blisters on the palm of my right hand. Each day a new blister or two added more incredible pain. Wrapping the hand in soft tissues kept the blisters clean but not protected from my daily activities at work. A skin specialist said he'd never witnessed anything like it on a hand, but it may have been shingles.

My lackluster immune system was sending me an S.O.S., but I didn't get the message. I just endured the pain and kept the hand lightly covered.

By Christmas Eve, everything felt like it was moving in slow motion, and I only recall part of the service in the cathedral.

The following evening, at Glen's family get-together, remains a blur. Later, I was shown a picture of myself sitting near the Christmas tree staring into space, thus proving I did indeed attend the event.

I developed a terrible cough that sapped my strength. Climbing the endless stairs to my third-floor apartment required stopping several times to catch my breath. I called my employer and received time off for my illness.

Although self-medicating with cough drops and flu symptom syrup, I rarely got out of my bed for several days. When my family called to check on me, they were concerned, but there was nothing they could do to support me, residing hundreds of miles away in California.

Glen worked long hours out of town. I was alone and dismayed, and my growing depression flirted with the possibility of a merciful death.

Aware of my increasingly dangerous situation, I managed to get down all the stairs and into my car. I drove to a nearby "Doc in the Box" and checked in. After being shown to a room, I lay down and fell asleep on a bench. They forgot about me, so by the time I wandered back into the hall and found the receptionist, it was dark.

The embarrassed physician checked my chest and temperature and wrote me two prescriptions. I managed to get to the first pharmacy, coughing and weak, and stood in the long line. Unfortunately, they could only fill one prescription and sent me to a second pharmacy for the other.

I must have filled the order and managed to get back up the stairs to my apartment, but I can't recall doing so.

Two months later, as I checked my coat pockets at the hospital discharge, my fingers discovered the two prescription vials. I hadn't taken any of the pills.

Miraculously, I caught Glen on his mobile phone and begged him to come to my assistance. He pleaded exhaustion, reminding me it was a long drive to my apartment, but reluctantly agreed to come sleep on my couch.

Thank God.

74

Nearing Death

Sometime in the middle of the night, my severe coughing woke me as I began choking on sticky fluid. I staggered to the bathroom and spit into the bowl. Red blood sprayed into the sink and onto the mirror. I looked up in horror and thought, *This can't be good!*

Panicked, I tried to awaken Glen, who grumbled sleepily but agreed to take me back to the medical clinic. We struggled as we descended the three flights of stairs, and Glen managed to help me into the car. Unable to catch my breath, I tried to remain upright in my seat.

As we drove into the dark parking lot, I distinctly felt the energy in my body start to leak from my head down towards my feet.

Shouting in a whisper, "I'm dying, I'm dying," I attempted to push the car door open as he slowed to find a parking space. Glen shouted a warning to me as he slammed on the brakes. He rushed to my opening door as I fell towards the pavement.

Nothingness enveloped me.

Glen scooped up my limp body and carried me awkwardly into the empty clinic lobby, shouting for help. The doctor on duty couldn't detect my pulse and demanded an ambulance from the attendant nurse.

I am told they revived me during the ambulance ride to an emergency room in a local hospital, where I would spend the next month in their critical care unit.

The influenza I contracted at Glen's concert had developed into pneumonia. As my condition worsened, I developed Acute Respiratory Distress Syndrome, aka ARDS, and was given a less than 40 percent chance of surviving.

As my weakened body lost ground, I required a tracheostomy and then the assistance of a ventilator.

Glen saved my physical life that night, but I left my body, nonetheless.

Sometime during the next three weeks, in a drug-induced coma, my soul slipped away from my body, my family, and life as I knew it.

PART IV
TOURING THE OTHER SIDE

75

It Begins

I didn't feel dead, only confused.

Total darkness and absolute silence were my only references.

Not daring to move, I waited.

The blackness morphed into a reddish glow, dragging with it a stinking heat. Acrid fog muffled moans and ungodly shrieks.

This can't be good.

Something was staring at me.

Like a blow, a voice thundered, "Do you know where you are?"

My mind raced, searching for some rational explanation, but part of me already knew. "Hell?" I whispered.

To my horror, the answer was an earsplitting, maniacal laugh.

The evil crept closer as I clamped shaking hands over my ears.

Panic surged in me, triggering the requirement for fight or flight.

Fighting was not an option.

I turned and ran.

76

First Impressions

The fog thinned as I took in a scene of epic destruction. Huge chunks of concrete with ruptured iron veins were strewn haphazardly in every direction. Remaining skyscrapers were eyeless skeletons. This unfortunate city resembled a nuclear war aftermath, complete with a fiery atmosphere of choking soot.

Short, dark shapes darted crab-like among the smoldering ruins, hissing like snakes.

Nearby, I noticed an opening in a splintered chunk of concrete. I bent low, sprinted to the hole, and tucked inside.

As I scanned the terrain from my makeshift hide-out, creatures peered at me from darkened places. They closed the gap between us, crouching from stone to stone. My terror mounted, and I glanced about for an escape route.

Gathering my courage, I accelerated through the burning debris and attempted to scale a concrete barrier. I clutched at the rusted rebar, but my feet slipped on the slick surface. Unable to escape, I watched helplessly as the creatures approached in increasing numbers.

"Who *are* you?" I shouted. No reply came, only echoes of ever-present wailing and painful screams.

The mob edged closer. In amazement, I realized they were has-been humans, mere skin and bones covered by rags.

We stared at each other; no bond apparent between us. Their unblinking bloodshot eyes were impossible to read.

Since no hope for them had been found in my arrival, the miserable band began to disperse and abandoned me to endless despair.

"No!" I shouted. "I will not give up. I will get out!"

Imploring them, I tempered my voice, "Look, while we're stuck here, let's at least help one another. Some could find food, others shelter…"

One soul interrupted me in an anguished voice, "We are all alone here."

He stared at me briefly, then shuffled to the vicinity of the others and melted into the timeless fog.

With sudden clarity, I realized I was once again the outcast "new kid."

77

Blackberry Battle

I was startled when the scene abruptly changed.

Before me towered a robed demon with the appearance of a judge. He proclaimed that I had but one chance to escape my fate. I was to be given a singular task, and when completed to his satisfaction, I would be released.

Hope lit a small spark in my chest. Unfortunately, as the soul-saving task was clarified, it became exceedingly clear that this charade was principally for their bizarre entertainment.

"Simply clear the field," it chuckled.

Before me materialized a flourishing and endless acreage of blackberry canes. Their robust growth of tangled hoops featured tough spines with surgically sharp tips. These monstrous plants hid succulent berries I had battled to obtain while on Earth. I was hyperaware of the impossibility of totally eradicating them.

An object mysteriously appeared in my hand, and I gazed down. Hope's spark fizzled out as I beheld a skimpy pair of round-tipped scissors kindergarten children use to cut paper.

Suppressing powerless rage, I bent to attempt cutting the woody vines at their source.

As the multitude of thorns tore at my flesh, I observed that as one branch was cut, another immediately grew in its place. With endless acres to cut, I rose and turned to glare at the judge.

The demon said, “You know you will never get out of here. Just give up—despair!” The repugnant laugh I had experienced upon arrival to this realm exploded again with added grotesque glee.

Something deep inside of me would not accept the demon’s debilitating promise. I knew, somehow, I would eventually be released, but *only* if I did not despair.

I continued cutting with those pitiful scissors, my hands and arms stinging and bloody.

I began to chant as loud as my quaking voice could manage, “I will not despair. I will get out of here. I will not despair…”

78

Beauty Parlor

In a split second I felt whisked to an incredibly unlikely scenario.

Before me, surrounded by total darkness, was a brightly lit stage setting of a faux beauty parlor. Several beautician's chairs were strategically placed nearly back to back, slanted at odd angles and on varying levels. The effect reminded me of a funhouse at the boardwalk.

Standing among the props, three familiar people awaited me.

The first, a female friend who I knew to be alive, greeted me warmly as if this were a perfectly normal meeting place, and then proceeded to tell me that I "looked awful."

My earthly friend looked beautiful and classy, as was her usual state.

Her favorite interests included the latest fashion, health food, exercise, and what she needed to make herself happy and secure. A relationship with this woman was fraught with worry about saying or doing her version of "the incorrect thing." Her sharp tongue and quick wit were renowned for slicing and dicing a person like an experienced sushi chef.

I was invited to take a seat in one of the chairs. Although they looked decidedly uncomfortable, I rested on the edge of the nearest one and eyed the new arrivals with intense suspicion. *Now what?*

I focused on the two beautifully appointed young men who were her best friends in the "real world."

Suddenly, as if on cue, the male duo launched into a pseudo-lecture detailing the correct use of certain cosmetics and surgical procedures required to look one's very best. They looked pointedly at me while making their case.

Something struck a familiar chord in me about the danger of putting transient outer beauty above the true value of inner beauty.

I felt compelled to speak up about this epiphany and began tentatively.

The men only paused briefly before laughing out loud, and then the trio jointly proceeded to ridicule me mercilessly. I was unable to insert my voice again because of the cacophony.

Saddened at the prospect of being alone once more, I exited the stage with a resolute sigh and was swallowed by the darkness.

79

Unwelcome Guest

I became conscious of trudging down an unfamiliar dirt path strewn with ankle-twisting rocks.

The smoky dark overhead merged with the arid desert scenery surrounding me. Occasionally, a small rise or fall of a few inches on the path would break the monotony.

My situation was not improving, and I now suffered from hunger, thirst, and a growing malaise. Struggling with the insidious desire to give up, I resolutely put one foot in front of the other.

I felt measurably revived as I spotted what appeared to be an outdoor dinner party ahead. Aromatic food was piled high on decorated serving tables.

Approaching a young woman in a Chinese sarong, I was amazed and heartened to recognize her as a living relative of mine. She was preparing her apparent husband a heaping plate of exotic food.

I greeted her warmly and pleaded for a pittance of the feast.

Even though I seemed to be recognized, she appeared annoyed at my request. Her answer was that there was no food to spare for me, as this feast was for "important people." Turning her back, she fussed about rearranging the various overflowing platters.

I was shocked and dismayed but reluctantly returned to the bleak path.

It seemed that nothing in this seemingly endless nightmare could surprise me now.

This wasn't correct.

80

The Clinic

A brilliantly lit hospital hallway scene stretched out before me. I blinked and tried to orient myself.

Accelerating in my direction was a huge being wielding an object resembling a prison guard's baton.

Forced to high alert, I glanced to the left and noticed a nondescript door ajar. Faint light escaped into the hall.

To my right, an open double door afforded me a view of countless white-gowned human backs.

A multitude of women lying flat on gurneys faced my direction with draped and splayed lower limbs. As heads bowed to a task between their vulnerable legs, debris was slopped onto nearby tables and into bins.

The manic activity and surrealistic visuals transfixed me.

As approaching footsteps ceased, I jerked my head forward and then upward. A looming demon received my full attention as it thundered a seemingly simple decree, "Your job is to enter the room on the right, retrieve all garbage, and deliver it into the room on the left."

It swelled to full height. “Starting now!”

After a brief hesitation, I quickly made my way to the room on the right and dared myself to enter.

A bloody raised hand motioned to me impatiently, and I willed myself to a gurney. A masked person placed a gruesome mass into my trembling arms and barked at me, “Get going!”

Dazed and horrified, I gently carried a ruined baby into the hallway. The demon lifted the thick black rod and growled a reminder, “Take it to the room on the left.”

The “room” was an unbelievably huge warehouse. My eyes beheld mountains of small broken bodies. I gagged at the stench and staggered backward with revulsion. Laying the bloodied bundle at the foot of the closest stack, I fled into the hall.

The unyielding demon indicated my expected next move by pointing the menacing rod to the room on the right.

Just before I entered, a female doctor, whose face mask hung from one ear, paused at the doorway and stared at me. Her once white garments were stained with blood and offal. I bent close to her and begged for an explanation. “What’s really going on in there?”

She hesitated, then whispered, “Those are indigent women who’ve been told they’re having a simple medical procedure, but their babies are being aborted.”

I didn't have the luxury of trying to figure out what that meant, so I took a chance before she could get away.

"We don't have to do this," I said under my breath. "We must refuse to do it. All of us."

She immediately distanced herself, gaped at me as if I were undeniably crazy, and sputtered, "You have no idea what they'll do to us if we even hint at refusing."

In an instant, the demon charged us in full attack mode. The doctor tore off to her assigned post.

Standing my ground as the distance between my tormentor and I lessened, I caused the beast to falter with my firm voice, "I can't do this. I won't do this!"

The demon's eyes blazed as it demanded my answer, "What kind of exquisite punishment have you earned for yourself now?"

Shutting my weary eyes, I awaited probable blows, or worse.

I received worse.

81

Rotten Shame

I wondered if the road I now found myself on was the same I traveled before but had no better choice than to keep moving. Maybe it was an immense treadmill.

It wasn't long before I noticed others heading in the same direction, and I didn't know what to expect as we entered a very congested area. Numerous shapes milled about, not slowing to interact with one another.

The dimness had faded to near black.

Not wanting to draw attention to myself, I attempted to keep my eyes on the ground, which no longer resembled a path, just muddy puddles and dirt. Occasionally, I would venture a glance at my companions.

All were in tatters. They appeared to be somewhat disfigured and were walking unsteadily. I couldn't control my eyes as they widened at the exposed flesh that was torn or rotting off. *Are they lepers?*

My spirit dropped to a new low, and my mind raced as to how I could escape this potentially dangerous situation.

As if the creatures could sense my fear, they slowed their shuffling.

Increasing my speed as much as I deemed prudent, I attempted to go around the thickest concentration of beings.

Unintelligible mutterings began irritating my ears as they turned in unison.

I've been spotted!

As they circled around me, I sought their faces and determined that they were male. Their evil chuckling and heavy breathing terrified me. They grew bolder as their prey oozed fear.

In unison, they began clawing at my clothes and pushing me one way, then another; cats playing with a mouse. One attacker snarled, saying that they all had AIDS and soon I would have it too!

As they closed in, I was shoved to the ground, and each seemed to take a turn with my body. I kicked and screamed, but no assistance was forthcoming. Their vicious sounds and rotten odors intensified my torture. The assaults continued, and I didn't have a prayer.

Bored or sated, I didn't know, but at last they began to withdraw with final painful kicks and cruel berating.

As the last of them turned to leave, he reconsidered and leaned to within inches of my battered face and said, "Now you will be like us...your AIDS will progress, your pain will increase, your flesh will rot, and the worst of it? You cannot die!"

With one last putrid laugh, he joined the others.

What am I to do now?

82

Cold as Hell

I pulled my torn clothing around me and attempted to stand. Hurting all over, I had no idea what would transpire next.

A confident female approached me and ordered, “Follow me. You’re one of us now.”

She led me to a small group of women, all as miserable looking as I felt. Their listless eyes, full of shame, stared resolutely at the ground.

With no alternative plan, I followed the mystery woman and my weary sisters single file into unknown territory.

As we proceeded, the town led into a desolate area. Our leader explained the facts. She had been assigned the role of madam in charge of the new whores of hell. We were assigned to a house in another territory and would begin our jobs upon arrival.

The last sliver of hope eked away from me. I noticed the temperature drop dramatically, and a fierce wind followed, whipping our hair into our faces and eyes as our bodies began to shiver uncontrollably.

Our tattered clothing proved little protection from the blizzard now swirling around us. Drifts became chest high, but somehow, we trudged slowly onward. I imagined enduring this frigid storm forever and was eerily grateful when we eventually bumped into a desolate log cabin.

It afforded no heat or furniture, and the wind howled through the uninsulated timbers.

Home sweet home.

Our leader seemed satisfied with the surroundings and declared in an insanely cheerful voice, “Now we wait for customers.”

My little family was unbelievably cold, hungry, and desolate.

As tortuous as my journey to date was, I felt compelled to ask our madam if this didn't seem like a particularly miserable day.

She quipped to my surprise, “Oh, it's Christmas on Earth today. Always the saddest 'time' in hell.”

After all I had been through, I couldn't resist.

I began singing a Christmas carol. My voice was a whisper, but I sang nonetheless, “Away in a manger…”

“Quiet!” the startled demon apprentice roared.

Another lost soul joined in, “no crib for a bed...”

The Madam shoved this woman aside as she charged my way.

The remaining women joined in, “the little lord…”

“Stop!” she screeched as she lunged at me.

I felt lost, abandoned, and doomed on Christmas.

Closing my eyes once again, I continued singing.

83

Glory, Glory

Unexpectedly, I felt the exhilaration of my entire being flooded with an abundance of love, peace, and joy! This indescribable feeling was akin to all the wonderful experiences of my life rolled into one, except infinitely more intense. An orgasm of the soul, for the want of a better description.

As I reveled in wonder and total happiness, I glanced around my new environment and spotted my dear friend Rick and gasped in astonishment.

He gave me a full grin, barely containing his own joy. I couldn't help but notice that his formerly gray hair was now brown and fuller. On Earth, he was expected to wear a suit and tie most of the time, but now he sported casual clothes and the tan sweater vest that I had given him last Christmas.

Only a few weeks earlier, Rick's physical condition was at a record low. Now he was not only chipper and fit; he was laughing at me!

"Oh," I reasoned in that unreasonable situation. "He doesn't know he's dead."

Rick let out a belly laugh and had a gleam in his eye that translated into, "I know something you don't know!"

Miraculously, our conversation was telepathic and flowed easily back and forth. Something strange was going on, and I took this as a clue.

I dared to consider: *If he's dead, then I'm dead!*

Glancing at Rick for feedback, I watched him do a silly Irish jig he usually performed when enjoying a really good time.

I tried on the phrase, "I'm dead." Once again. "I'm dead, and I'm in heaven!"

My whole being rejoiced at the wondrous prospect. *Wow! I made it!*

In the utter joy of that moment, I had no thought whatsoever of my hideous journey through hell or my fifty-three years of life on Earth. My focus was on Rick.

I was puzzled. *Here I am in heaven with Rick, but what about angels singing and the rest of that promised stuff?*

Reviewing my surroundings slowly this time, I observed that everything—the walls, floor, and ceiling—were a dazzling white.

I noticed a medium-sized arched doorway a short distance behind Rick and a massive architect's table off to my right.

Maybe that doorway leads to the rest of heaven and God… Was Rick instructed to keep me from entering?

In the middle of the tall table lay an oversized book opened about halfway. The huge pages appeared to have information on them, and they resembled a plat map or a massive ledger.

As a faint memory of Rick showing me something in that book drifted into my consciousness, I recalled being distressed at our discussion of it and responding, "Oh, no, that will be too hard. I just want to stay here with you."

This was disturbing and foreboding.

Rick moved slowly toward me, careful that we didn't touch. He looked into my eyes and gently said, "Now, Rach, you have too much left to do."

As it dawned on me that I was being sent back to life on Earth, I totally freaked out!

"NO!" I cried. Clenching my fists, I stomped my right foot like a thwarted two-year old.

It was to no avail.

84

Heading Back

The springtime air, warmed by the sunlit day, invited deep breaths.

Nestled near a flower-infused meadow, a frisky rivulet polished flat stones and whispered as it ran.

It wasn't heaven, but it was heavenly.

I felt compelled to follow the water as it gently twisted and sloped down a verdant hillside.

As the stream gradually descended, the walls of embedded river rock rose protectively on both sides. This natural gateway encouraged my continuation downstream, but as the opening narrowed, I was forced to step carefully from one flat stone to the next.

Rounding a turn, I was surprised to encounter an older woman standing on the left side of a sandy bank. I paused, filled with curiosity.

She greeted me with a welcoming smile and an enthusiastic wave. As the woman began speaking to me in a foreign language, she offered me some handmade linen pieces. I tried to explain that I didn't understand, but I accepted the items. This made her smile, and she pointed for me to continue downstream.

Tucking the items under my arm, I proceeded over the slippery rocks. As the stream hooked to the right, a small island of sand appeared. A second older woman sat rocking in an ancient chair, a quilt on her lap. In the same foreign tongue, she stood, smiled broadly, and presented me with the quilt. With her hand gently on my shoulder, she pointed my way downstream.

The items were awkward to carry, and I sighed when greeted by a third woman. She draped a delicate negligee trimmed with handmade lace at the cuffs and collar over my shoulder.

Although laden with gifts, I accepted her enthusiastic hug.

Suddenly, I clearly understood, even though I could not interpret their words, the women were supplying me with a dowry and welcoming me as a future bride into their family. I took them to be Scandinavian but wasn't sure.

At what would be my last encounter, a final woman gave me a small, rolled-up sheet of paper and said in English, "Give this to Glen and tell him you must live together." As I began to move forward, she added, "Don't forget to give him the paper and tell him…"

PART V:
RECOVERY

85

Crash Landing

Bright light stung my dazed eyes. When I attempted to twist from the pain, I discovered my head was fixed in place.

Several people were milling about in a small room where I appeared to be bed-ridden. Straining my eyeballs to the left, I recognized my son-in-law, who appeared startled as he announced, "Mother is back."

My eyes rolled right as my daughter said with disappointment, "I wanted to be the first thing she saw when she woke up." My mother's cry of joy reached my ears as I looked above my blanketed feet.

I was back alright—and wasn't happy about it.

Time seemed warped somehow, and I felt as if I had been away from my family for a couple of years. They surrounded me, all talking at once. Uncomfortably hot, I couldn't move at all. Something invaded my throat so that I couldn't speak.

I asked myself: *Why have they wrapped me in duct tape and turned the room into a sauna?*

After inducing my coma, a physician ordered a halt to my weekly estrogen patches, so now

I experienced severe hot flashes beneath the smothering blankets. As my mother approached, asking if I was cold and hovering with an additional covering, I could only blink like crazy.

This situation was akin to hell, but these people seemed to like me. I lay trapped, confused, totally vulnerable, and extremely frightened.

Pushing the others away, Lauren leaned in close. "Mom," she said slowly as if talking to a young child, "you have been very sick. You have been asleep for a long time, but now you are going to get better."

She would be reiterating this numerous times in the coming days. My brain was fuzzy with drugs and disuse and it couldn't hold a thought.

Lauren's explanation gave me no comfort. My recent heaven expatriation was a complex situation that I couldn't explain to them, even if it was physically possible.

In hindsight, my inability to communicate at that moment was a blessing. My mind was screaming: *If you people really cared about me you wouldn't have brought me back!*

Such ingratitude on my part would have been unthinkable to a rational mind.

Slowly, I was able to comprehend the physical basics. After contracting the flu and developing pneumonia, I had been placed into a medically induced coma for almost three weeks. Careful monitoring of the ventilator kept me alive. In addition to a tracheostomy, I had been intubated for liquid nourishment.

I currently weighed eighty-seven pounds and had lost most of my muscle mass, thus my faux paralysis. I could barely move the pointer finger on my left hand, and I could blink my eyes. Nothing else worked. The gradual comprehension of my new reality devastated me.

My family and doctors continued to be elated. Repeatedly, they proclaimed my survival miraculous and me lucky to be alive.

Lucky? I mourned. No, only angry and cheated at the loss of my eternity in heaven.

I was terrified by my physical deterioration and the prognosis for a limited recovery. Upon overhearing the attending physician caution my family of the possible extent of my brain damage, and doubts of my walking or driving a car again, my heart withered inside me. Relentless despair stalked me anew.

They discussed my future rehabilitation and care in hushed and worried tones. Since it seemed unlikely for me to live on my own for an undetermined amount of time, my future loomed as a complicated problem for my family.

My mom attempted to cheer me with her success story of establishing a world-wide prayer chain for my survival. She said I would never know all the people that prayed for me daily or ever be able to thank adequately the ones that I did know.

At that moment, however, I cursed their prayers and generous efforts.

86

Suffering in Silence

In the midst of monitoring my many attendant bottles and machinery, a nurse got my nasal feeding tube caught on her sweater button. As she leaned behind me to tap a bottle, I noticed a tug on my tube.

Unable to speak, I made some guttural noises, but she took no notice. As she moved deeper into the tangle of cords, I felt the tube being drawn from my throat. Panicking, I grunted and moaned, trying to catch her attention.

Intent on her process, she whipped around and asked gruffly, "What?"

Zing... The feeding tube was yanked from my stomach, through my throat, out my nose, and hung from her sweater button. Boy, did that sting!

She looked into my shocked eyes and picked up the tube. Without an apology or an ounce of sympathy, she came at me, intending to put the tube into its proper place.

My mind was clear enough to realize this intrusion was usually done under anesthesia, and I was wide awake!

Uhnnnn! and a small shake of my head was all I could muster, but my intent was clear.

She leaned close to my face and muttered, "Well, you better learn to eat, then." She tossed the tube into a trash receptacle and left the room.

As I lay alone and mute, I imagined her as a good candidate for a demon someday and wondered how many incapacitated people were bullied because they were unable to report their abuse.

Lauren volunteered to be responsible for teaching me to open my mouth, accept soft food on a spoon, and the exceedingly difficult process of swallowing.

The look on my grown daughter's face was a mimic of my first attempts to feed her in infancy. I found it amusing and felt immensely grateful for her tender ministrations. I disliked oatmeal, so we started with applesauce. After two months of only intravenous saline and fake vanilla liquid down my nose, it tasted delicious.

The other misfortune I recall while existing in the CCU involved the dreaded bedpan. After my catheter was removed, I lay on a lined pad used in baby cribs. Thin as a small child, I was twisted to one side to remove and replace the liners when soiled.

As I recovered, someone on the nursing staff had the bright idea that I would welcome a cold hard plastic pan placed under my limp spine. The process was very painful since I was literally skin and bones.

It did not help that the nurse placed the pan under me, returned the many layers of heavy blankets, and then forgot me.

Over an hour, or more, I lay helpless and silent in abject pain. I stared at the wall clock, attempted mental telepathy with the nurses I could see in the hall, and silently screamed in agony.

When the nurse finally returned, she saw the tears running down my face and asked, "What's wrong?" When I couldn't reply, but just let out a sob, she remembered the pan and rushed to remove it.

I was roughly turned on my side as she peeled back the blankets, and the bedpan was removed. Her fingers inspected the deep ruts in my back as she murmured aloud that the skin didn't appear to be broken.

With no apology, she returned me to my back and took the bedpan from the room with her.

My daughter passed the nurse in the doorway, and nothing was said. Lauren came to my bedside and noticed my crying, and she asked vainly what was wrong. Although I vowed to remember the nurse's name, this wasn't possible with my muddled brain.

There is so much needless hell on Earth. I learned much while in my vulnerable and helpless state. I learned compassion, empathy, and to pay attention to the needs of others. We are indeed our brother's and sister's keepers, like it or not.

87

Reconnecting

My mom and Lauren devised a new communication aid. Up to this time, when they asked me questions, I would answer with one blink of my eyes for "no" and two for "yes." The cumbersome exchange of information remained tedious and unreliable.

With expectant smiles, they proudly held a large homemade Ouija board before my face next to my only working finger. After asking me a question, they held the board so that I could "tap" out a reply. Unfortunately, they held the board too high and my weakened hand could only reach the lower level of letters.

As I struggled to form a word, they puzzled, "Z-N-X-C?"

My exhausted hand fell to my chest. Always the ones to default to humor no matter what the severity of the situation, my daughter attempted to pronounce, "ZNXC?"

My mother said, "Maybe she learned another language while she was in the coma!"

Peals of laughter ensued.

I wasn't in a humorous mood. One of the worst things about hell is it quashes your sense of humor. Without it, despair is just around the corner.

After that failed attempt at communication, my inventive head nurse procured an attachable device for my trach apparatus. Soon I would be speaking like a robot. I was delirious with joy!

Instructed to force air from my stomach and out my throat, my first enthusiastic attempt disengaged the device and launched it across the room, just missing my nurse.

Experimenting with control of the pressure proved successful, and I was vocal after a month of being "on mute." The effect was creepy, but miraculous! I practiced for hours before sleeping that night.

The next morning, Lauren arrived and offered a cheery, "Good morning!"

I replied with a verbal greeting of my own. She froze and stared at me, then looked around for an explanation. I pointed to the device at my throat and chatted weirdly through labored breaths. We cried with relief and joy.

All day long, I was able to startle my family and visitors. I tend to be on the loquacious side, and this technological assistance escalated the process of becoming me again.

88

Opening Up

After several inquiries from my family and Glen about my experience in "the coma," I attempted to explain my confusion and fear of hell and my elation with Rick in heaven.

The need to share my experiences was thwarted by gasps of horror or shakes of their heads. They murmured, "You were on a lot of drugs" and "Forget those nightmares; it didn't really happen."

The only verification emerged as my mom whispered to me soon after I awoke in the hospital. She asked excitedly, "Did you see Rick? Were you talking to him?" Unfortunately, I was mute at the time and could only blink my eyes and shake my head a bit.

She continued, her voice rising, "I knew it! I was watching your sleeping face, when all of a sudden it seemed to sort of glow, and you tried to smile. Then your lips moved like you were talking to someone. No one was here with me, and I started shouting, 'Send her back, Rick, you can't have her yet. Send her back!'"

That was the good news and the bad news. I was so angry at her but thankfully wasn't able to rebuke her.

Two months later, after complaining to her one too many times about how distraught I was about being sent back, I added, “If I ever come this close to death again, don’t even think of ‘saving’ me.”

She immediately quipped, “Don’t worry; we won’t!”

After all she and the others had been through on my account, I didn’t blame her.

89

Angels and Willpower

With little muscle mass on my rag doll body, I could not sit erect unaided. My critical care unit doctor ordered me tied to a chair for prescribed minutes every day to strengthen my spine.

This activity brought on muscle cramping and severe pain in my back. I could only endure it for short periods at a time. When they finally decided to place my chair in front of a small window, I stared happily into the hospital parking lot. This was my only enjoyable activity, and it helped mitigate the pain and lengthen the sittings.

Stabilized, and no longer welcome in the CCU where I resided for almost a month, the insurance company became involved.

The question of whether to send me to a convalescent home or a hospital rehabilitation facility was discussed by my doctors and the insurance representative. The opinion of the insurance company was I wasn't worth the expense of a proposed rehabilitation that in all likelihood could not be achieved.

I demanded a personal interview and met with a very professional insurance agent. She observed a bed-ridden, fifty-three-year-old woman who looked like a refugee of some death camp and didn't see any possibilities worth their investment.

I pleaded my case, explaining this "hiccup" in my life didn't define the real me.

A fighter and a survivor for half a century, nothing about my spirit had changed, only intensified. With a promise to overcome my handicaps, I'd be a model for others.

She didn't say much, just thanked me for my time and indicated she would file a report.

My family, nurses, and I waited, knowing my fate rested in her hands and in the pockets of the insurance company. If I were sent to a convalescent facility, I'd need to recover the best I could with a modicum of assistance. It was not a viable alternative, and we all prayed for a miracle.

When the determination letter came, my father needed to read it to us twice.

They agreed to pay for up to four weeks of hospital rehabilitation, with the stipulation that all my doctors (physical therapists, occupational therapists, pulmonary physician, etc.) met weekly and filled out the insurance company's required forms concerning my progress. If I did not meet the minimum requirements for the week, the insurance money would stop.

This was a blessing and a challenge, adding more stress as well as hope to our weary efforts.

"Whoops—one more thing," my dad warned. To qualify for this offer, I must "walk unattended for ten steps."

My biggest achievement since returning from the dead was to sit in a wheelchair. There was no way I could walk one step, much less ten. One by one, we wilted—except for my head nurse. He had seen me this far and wasn't about to give up.

The next morning, he arrived with a plan. My family and I listened intently as he insisted we had a slim chance. As his outrageous idea unfolded, our shoulders started slumping, and some people, including me, sighed.

"All we have to do is take her to the exercise room and put her on the parallel bars."

"I can't hold myself up on the parallel bars," I whined. My family shook their heads in agreement.

He continued, "We'll drape her arms over the bars up to her armpits, then we'll all shout encouragement as she drags her feet one at a time for ten steps."

All eyes were on me. This was our only chance. "Right," I said. "Piece of cake."

My nurse booked the exercise room for privacy and asked another of my nurses to join us and confirm completion of my impossible feat.

The two nurses lifted me from the wheelchair and placed me between the bars, then lowered my frail body so that I hung from my armpits, head drooping, with my feet toe-down behind me. From this position, I was expected to commence my ten-step walk. It was not an inspiring sight.

My family acknowledged the fear and dread in my eyes but came through with our family good humor, shouting, "You can do it!" and "Go, go, go…"

From the sidelines, my nurse raised a hand and pointed upward, "ONE!"

Attempting to be a good sport, I focused all my attention on my right foot. Desperately praying, I begged my leg to move forward.

By the shouts of my audience, I knew that something happened. Millimeter by millimeter, my foot magically edged forward to a place that earned the shout, "TWO!"

I only recall now it seemed like an eternity laboring down that long stretch. A few times there were exclamations of alarm when my arms started slipping through the bars, and the nurses jumped into action to reposition them.

By the grace of God, I finally heard shouts of joy and thunderous applause.

Sweating profusely, I looked around at my fans and asked, "Now, how far do I have to fly?"

I was on my way to Phase II.

90

Rehab Blues

Although happy about advancing to the rehab facility, I was reluctant to leave my head nurse and predictable daily routine. I was still emotionally fragile and dependent.

Between the preparation for the ambulance ride and the frenetic energy of the EMTs caring for me, I could only stare out the window of the vehicle and hope for the best. I watched as the haven where I had been reborn faded into the distance.

My new abode was quiet since it was Sunday, and the only alarm I felt was in passing a mirror in my assigned room. As they rolled my chair toward my awaiting bed, I glanced into the mirror and was shocked and saddened to see a decrepit old woman in a wheelchair.

My family and Glen had been successful in keeping my appearance a non-issue. I knew I was thin, but that lady was a living skeleton. Her hair was thin and stringy, with eyes sunken and dull. She was so old. Words cannot describe the dismay and revulsion I felt realizing the image was mine.

I loved my family for their sympathy and courage and the ability to see me as I used to be—pretty and healthy. I felt grateful for not seeing my image up to now.

Can I ever really be myself again? Is this all an elaborate and fruitless dream?

The book *Still Me* by Christopher Reeve, read by me only months before, drifted into my mind. Recalling Mr. Reeve's fight with near-total paralysis, I rallied slightly. Page after page of his courage streamed through my mind like a movie, and I realized how fortuitous it was for me to have finished that book. Bolstered by the remembrance of his smiling face, I realized that I, too, was still me. Like so many of my ancestors, I had great genes and would prevail.

Allowing myself a smidgen or two of sympathy, I decided that if my loved ones came this far and still thought I was worth it, I wouldn't let them down.

I had thirty days in which to do it.

91

Race Against Time

Early Monday morning brought my introduction to rehab. The admitting nurse efficiently performed her patient intake duties. Height, weight, abilities, and inabilities dutifully noted, she placed a gadget in my right hand and folded my fingers around it.

The metal tube instantly dropped to the floor and rolled under our table. This brought a surprised look, and the nurse disappeared to the floor.

Lauren asked the purpose of the instrument. The nurse explained the device's use was to measure my hand and finger strength. Since my initial movement was in my left finger, we asked her to take the reading in my "strong" hand.

This time the nurse lightly held my fingers in place and ordered me to "squeeze it" with all my strength. I grimaced and groaned and squeezed until I was exhausted.

After the nurse checked the numbers, she frowned and said, "I need you to try again and really squeeze tightly this time."

Lauren and I exchanged puzzled looks, but I dutifully allowed the object to be re-inserted.

As my fingers were replaced, the two women encouraged me with reverberating, "Squeeze, squeeze!" and "Harder, harder!"

I gave it my all and fell back against my wheelchair, grinning at my efforts.

The nurse checked the reading, excused herself, and ducked into a back room for five minutes, then returned. She explained that her supervisor requested she enter the reading and move on to another test.

Daily, the therapists and I faced daring accomplishments, such as turning over on my side, over to my stomach, and then returning to my back; learning to climb stairs; and going from lying flat on my back to standing upright.

My muscles and brain had lost contact with each other, and these seemingly "natural" abilities baffled me until the therapist "talked me through" each increment of the movements.

Climbing the set of practice stairs proved hardest, and once at the top of six stairs, I couldn't figure how to descend. As I grew tired and weaker, I panicked. A fall down the stairs would undo all of my previous labors and maybe kill me. I shouted to the therapist to save me.

He calmly began, "Hold on to the banister and look down. Pick up your right knee and move it forward. Bend your left knee slightly and lower your right foot to the step."

I was in tears, but I completed the descent. I hated physical therapy.

I was wheeled to my room for a rest each afternoon before dinner. Once, after arriving, and helped to stand facing my bed, I dismissed the orderly. Then I challenged myself to "climb into bed" instead of my usual regimen of "sit, lie on your side, roll to your back. Stare at the ceiling."

The thought of leaping into the clean bed sheets on hands and knees, crawling to the pillow, and flopping over on my back was akin to a siren's song. It almost begat a dirge.

I had learned to lift one knee and put it on the bed. It seemed logical to turn slowly and face the head of the bed, then to reach one hand in front of me, lean forward, and plant the other hand on my bed.

So, I did, sort of.

As I hovered facing the pillow, my weakened arms collapsed and propelled me forward, face-first into the pillow. With my arms limp at my sides I couldn't move and wasn't having too much luck breathing either.

In a split second, disaster had struck. As I struggled to move my head to the side for air, I wiggled everything, hoping my body would respond somewhere with a helpful movement.

A vision of a staff member finding my cold body in this stupid situation and explaining it to my family kept me fighting. Miraculously, I finally smelled disinfectant instead of polyester foam.

I calmed myself and inched the fingers of my free hand to the side of the bed to the safety railing. I'm not sure how I managed to escape; it's all a blur. An angel must have been on duty.

The next day at physical therapy, my nurse asked what I'd like to learn next. Without a pause, I requested, "Crawling."

I now appreciate babies' struggles with this activity. It takes an enormous amount of concentration and patience, but so worth the effort. This was the hardest movement I had to relearn.

92

Dining Out

My low weight inhibited a return to normalcy. Subsisting on a liquid diet for over three weeks caused my appetite to disappear. I was encouraged (forced) to take my meals with the other "inmates," as we called ourselves in rehab.

I dressed down for dinner in a fetching hospital gown and matching robe. To complete the ensemble, I sported toe-to-thigh compression socks under knee-length, cotton argyles.

However, as a hunched, skeletal crone, with straggly hair and a grimace for a smile, the "new kid" was on the bottom rung of the ladder when it came to "at least I'm better off than that person."

My tablemates' cautious glances and whispered pitying comments stung.

A hideous cough forced phlegm through the trached hole in my throat, and it was an ordeal for me to clean it at the table. Feeling like a child with an unchecked runny nose did not improve my social status or their appetites.

The greatest percentage of the populace, in for strokes and complications of diabetes, required restricted diets. Most of the patients were overweight.

They stared forlornly at their pitiful portions of healthy food while I was burdened with a large plate of sliced beef and a mound of mashed potatoes and gravy. The sight of all that heavy food caused me to be nauseous, but my tablemates salivated.

I wanted a slice of pizza or a taco, and frequently a family member would venture out to procure one as a treat.

A lovely plump nurse fussed over my barely touched food and offered to sneak me a generous slice of cheesecake each evening. I never even saw the cheesecake. Glen found it first and thought it was a snack for him. He gained ten pounds while I was in the hospital.

93

Angel Wrap

Since being forced to a mostly inactive life in that first hospital bed, my bored mind too often drifted to recollections of the demons and the prison in which they tortured me. The haunting was insistent, and I feared dying in my sleep with a resultant rerun in hell.

The prescription aids in the CCU afforded me sleep, but the rehabilitation hospital offerings were insufficient. I begged my family and boyfriend to sit with me at all hours so that I might be safe.

After a long watch with me, Lauren was inspired to "wrap me in angels" to give her time to use the restroom or grab a cup of coffee.

Standing at the foot of my bed, waving her arms and hands in a circular motion, she would pronounce her intentions for my protection. "I am wrapping you in angels, Mom," she said, "and nothing can harm you." Desperate as I was, I clung to the belief that this was true.

One night after Lauren had completed a "wrap," she tried to sleep in a chair pushed up to the side of my bed. With her tired eyes closed, she soon heard a sound like "tinkling bells and babies laughing." Barely opening one eye, she saw little bubbles of light tumbling and swirling all around my sleeping body, as if playing a game of tag.

A few seconds passed as Lauren held her breath. With the eventual exhale, she must have been noticed because the vision and sounds disappeared, and I awoke from a deep sleep. Lauren was beside herself with joy and easily convinced me of the miracle.

94

A Step Back

Just as my condition appeared to improve, they discovered large blood clots in both of my thighs as a result of being bedridden. The technician using the ultrasound on my legs shook her head and told me she'd never seen anything like it.

She hoped out loud the blood thinners I was receiving would safely dissolve them. "If they break into bits," she explained dispassionately, "they might travel to your brain or heart, causing stroke or death."

How much more of this distress must I endure to get all the way out of hell? I pondered.

This bad news was soon coupled with the fact that my other lung was collapsing. The pulmonologist decided to put a chest tube drain through my breast, between the lung and rib cage.

The procedure would be performed under a local anesthetic in my hospital bed before an audience of other doctors and nurses. Since use of the procedure was rare, the staff were anxious to witness the event.

I wondered if there would be popcorn.

Terrified and anxious, I stared as ten or more strangers crowded into my room and eyed me with clinical curiosity. Glen handed me my eye shades to block out the sight and started my tape recording of Yanni to fill the room with soothing music.

I barely noticed a lessening of my fear.

Lying still on my formerly safe bed, I felt like a living cadaver at autopsy. My doctor slowly explained each step in advance, alerting the students of each movement and causing me to flinch with anticipation of pain. His matter-of-fact instructions for me to relax went unheeded.

"First," he said, "the injection of a local anesthetic into the edge of the right breast near the rib cage." He stabbed and then dug deeper. A tear made its way down the side of my face as I tried to meditate by slowing my breathing. I was determined to be brave and prayed for courage.

Next, the surgeon explained the need for a certain type of scalpel and palpation of the area to locate the exact spot to cut a hole for the tubing, including the depth of the incision.

I wanted to scream and leap from the bed but instead concentrated on Glen's hand holding mine tightly, and begged God to help me.

The sound of the knife entering my chest was faint but grotesque, and I focused on the doctor's explanation of finding the correct depth to avoid thinking about his actions.

He wiggled the blade gently back and forth until he was satisfied with the probe, then quickly removed the dagger, accepted the length of thin, flexible hose from an assistant, and began feeding it into my chest cavity. His unhurried dialogue allowed me and the medical students to keep up with his experienced hands.

After several attempts to place the drain at the proper depth, a gurgling of air or some other magic event told him of a successful placement, and I praised God that there wouldn't be a need for a second try.

Polite applause and audible sighs of relief emanated from the peanut gallery. They had been more invested in my plight than I first thought.

The hose in my chest was taped in place, and a small bottle was attached at the end about twelve inches below the hole. Immediately it began siphoning out a murky liquid from the cavity, and it dripped into the bottle. The doctor hoped all the liquid gathering inside my chest would be displaced to allow my lung room to expand and reattach itself to the proper place.

That's all my freaked-out mind was able to remember anyway.

It was several days before the bottle showed an acceptable amount of fluid and the x-rays were positive. I had gotten used to the bottle dangling at my groin. I reported to my family that it felt like I had a penis and joked that I was going to miss it after it had performed its duty.

I didn't.

Later, as I asked Jesus some hard questions concerning why I was brought back in this condition, the nasty word “despair” entered my discouraged mind. Even though I made it through hell, this whole Earth situation certainly challenged my trust in God.

What was the point of all this?

95

Inquiring Minds

In the wee hours, unable to sleep and afraid to dream, I wrestled with God.

He was stronger and smarter, but I had free will and I wanted answers.

As the Voice and I squared off, I got in the first jab. "Say, you might have noticed that I have been praying like hell and you seem to have gone deaf."

"I'm asking You to humor me here," I continued. "What is the purpose of letting my baby die, my soul-wrenching divorces, a rape without recourse, my dearest friend dying a horrible death, and now this hideous physical mess I'm in? Just askin'!"

As I mentally crossed my arms and glared at The Almighty, I heard a chuckle, then a guffaw.

"Well, funny you should ask," came the patient reply. "You may have heard that I'm known for my 'mysterious ways,' so answering your questions isn't my usual modus operandi. But, let me share a few insights, since you asked so nicely."

The Voice continued, "I know you've heard the joke about this life only being a test, and if this had been a real life, you would have been given instructions on where to go and what to do. You keep a copy of that saying posted above your computer."

I really did.

"Spirits go to Earth as people, and to other planets, to learn lessons. They choose what they wish to learn and arrange for many of their soulmates to meet up with them along the journey in order to assist each other. They do their best and return home to be with Me.

"They can go as often as they like.

"I've sent many good souls over the millennia to be examples and to share spiritual teachings to make the journey easier. A lot of folks think they just made it harder—"

"But, do you mean—" I interrupted and was interrupted in turn.

"Rach, you chose this life, these challenges, the people you have interacted with, and the upcoming events you will experience. I understand when you call on Me to save you from your own pre-life choices, but if I changed the course of any of those events, it would thwart your original intentions."

"As you mentioned, you have free will, and I don't interfere. I do, however, shower you with grace to keep you going and love you dearly for your courage and tenacity. You've taken a lot on in the life you chose this time around."

"Oh," I said. "Great talk. Thanks for your time. Love you!"

96

Weaning Woes

After too brief a time, the nurses ordered my exhausted family members to return to their respective homes so I could acclimate to a new reality and commence my journey to self-sufficiency. I was devastated and afraid and begged them not to abandon me.

When they departed, I prayed for the strength to continue without their vital support.

Even when I did manage to fall asleep, the inhalation therapist glided into my room in the middle of the night, removed the cap on my trach tube, and squirted salt water down my throat to make me cough. This helped bring up the remaining glue in my lungs. His procedure caused convulsive coughing and a lot of pain.

I hated his midnight calls. No wonder he wore silent shoes; he needed the element of surprise to be able to perform his terrible task. As I recovered, I demanded he only come in the daytime. The nurse said my anger was a good sign. I was getting better.

Glen came to the hospital after work for the two months I was hospitalized. After my family was banished, he brought me tapes of soothing music and headphones to assist in my learning to sleep again unguarded. Glen's devotion was evident throughout my ordeal, and my family and nurses thought it helpful for my recovery.

Because one lung had already collapsed, and the ARDS damage was severe, I was subjected to twice-daily chest x-rays. I remember being wheeled into the spacious, cold room in my hospital "nightie" and being told to "hop up on the table" by a clueless technician.

HOP?

In my breathless and hushed voice, I would ask for assistance, and together we would attempt to raise me up to spread me out slowly in the desired positions. The pain that accompanied lying on a frozen and solid surface was excruciating. It was nearly impossible to lie still for the procedure between my shivering and sniveling.

One afternoon, as I sat parked in the hallway awaiting an orderly to return me to my room, I watched the people around me. A woman with a young daughter stood in my line of sight at the receptionist's window.

I ordinarily kept my eyes down because people did not make eye contact with me. I seemed invisible.

As the woman tried to solve a problem with the receptionist, the little girl clung to her mother's leg. With a finger in her mouth, she eyed me cautiously.

I was seen! Thrilled, I attempted a smile, but with a body of skin and bone, a grimace was all I could offer.

The small eyes widened as she let out a shriek and began to cry. Her mom looked down at her, and then at me. I felt horrified and ashamed. The mother attempted to comfort her daughter and said for my benefit, "It's not polite to stare, honey."

Grateful when the orderly arrived at that moment, I contemplated the situation and asked myself which was worse—to be invisible or to be seen?

I was blessed with a lesson. In the future, I would seek out the eyes of those in wheelchairs, and other downcast individuals, make eye contact, and add a smile. If appropriate, I would also add a friendly "Hi."

We all want to be "seen."

97

A Big Decision

Glen and Me in Rehab

As soon as I had been able to talk, I carefully told Glen of the messages from the ladies at the stream. He admitted to his Scandinavian heritage.

I highlighted their insistence that we live together. He was troubled by their request, and I was anxious at what he might think about this unusual missive from the "other side."

Glen shared his reluctance to live together unless we were married. I could not in my wildest dreams expect someone to marry me in my unknowable state. It seemed like an impossible situation.

I asked God to guide me and Glen. With multiple marriages and divorces between us, another failed marriage was to be avoided at all costs. Glen told me he would pray about it, too.

Six weeks later, in the rehabilitation hospital, while two nurses were in attendance of my needs, Glen proposed. One nurse exclaimed happily as she clapped her hands, and the other covered her face and began to cry.

I cried too and said, "Yes." Our prayers appeared to be answered.

Rehab rules dictated I attain a weight of 100 pounds. I got to 99 pounds and was stuck there. Finally, one of the nurses put a toe on the scale to help me achieve the goal.

The Occupational Therapist required that I prove capable of cooking, so I made packaged chocolate chip cookies and lured multiple staff members into the kitchen lab with the aroma.

When I could make my own bed and feed myself, I could finally go home with my fiancé.

PART VI

NOW WHAT?

98

A New Reality

On February 28, 2000, after two full months in hospitals, I tentatively left the nest.

As I was saying goodbye to my wonderful therapists, the admitting nurse came to compliment me on my accomplishments and wish me success in my new life.

Her eyes grew moist as she recalled my initial testing. Our meeting occurred on the first day of her new job. She had consulted her supervisor after my hand strength test because despite my valiant efforts, the machine had not registered any movement at all.

My overwhelming disabilities caused her to break into tears with pity, and she feared she wouldn't be able to help me. The young woman doubted her choice of career at the enormousness of my plight and asked to be taken off my case. The wise supervisor told her to return to her patient and to do her best.

Watching my tenacity gave the fledgling nurse strength, and witnessing my substantial recovery restored her hope. She wanted to thank me for the opportunity to assist me in our joint journey. I felt joy at her words and the beginnings of feeling a purpose in my struggles.

Maybe I could help people as a Heaven Expat after all.

As my primary doctor released me from the rehabilitation hospital, he looked at me sternly with folded arms and shook his head. He said, "I don't believe that you are alive, much less recovering so well. I will never understand it."

"Prayer," I answered simply.

"Yah, sure," he said offhandedly. "But I really don't understand it."

I smiled.

For the first two months, my fiancé and I stayed with his family. Glen had been living in their large home after moving up from out of state, but soon we would be renting a home nearby.

After my first non-hospital shower, I pulled a brush through my hair and was startled as clumps of it detached. I discovered the soles of my feet and palms of my hands began to shed thick layers of skin. They eerily peeled half-way down each hand and foot like a banana skin, with the remaining skin still attached.

I thought I was having a nightmare, but it was real.

A phone call to the doctor's office informed us that in severe illnesses like mine, the body sheds unnecessary parts of the body, especially at the extremities. I felt like I was falling apart.

During the day, Glen and his family spent long hours at work. The present peace and quiet of my makeshift home starkly contrasted with my frenetic hospital environment, and I felt anxious.

With my family and friends residing in other states, my only personal contact with them was infrequently via the telephone. Too much alone time allowed my dark thoughts of "the other side" to reemerge and I moped about the empty house in fear and desolation.

I rejoiced when I received a rare telephone call from Tanoshi, and after assuring him of my continued existence on the planet, I entrusted him with a secret.

His English was still superior to my Japanese, but I struggled to express my sincere desire to be dead. I missed heaven and I missed being with Rick, I confided. So much so, it caused me continuing emotional and spiritual agony.

Tanoshi paused, and I feared our connection had severed, but he said softly: "I miss Rick, too. Velly, velly much."

His displacement of the "r" for the "l" made me start to cry as I recalled Tanoshi with Rick and me as a happy family unit. The loss of my prior life avalanched down on me and I felt suffocated, welcoming death.

Tanoshi reminded me, "I wanted to die, but you said, 'No!'"

I knew he could hear my sobbing, but he bravely continued, "Now I say 'no' to you, host mother."

Tanoshi had become a successful writer, and I knew I must find the courage to continue my life, too. He felt like an angel to me that day, and his love and confidence gave me a reason to live.

99

Feet On The Ground

To keep my mind distracted, I concentrated on physically improving my shriveled body. Still only able to take a few wobbly steps before needing a rest to catch my breath, I began a self-imposed regimen.

Walking the length of the inside of the small house was a good start, and I increased the laps slowly.

Gradually, I worked up the courage to go outside and to the end of a long driveway and back. Eventually, I would walk a block, then two, down our quiet, wooded street. Day after day, I extended myself.

Walking in nature proved the best exercise for strengthening my body, increasing my lung power, and lifting my spirits.

Because of the large blood clots, my doctor put me on blood thinning medication for six months. After I was well into my walking exercises, the pulmonologist asked to check my oxygen readings, which had been ridiculously low for a long time.

I decided to surprise the doctor and didn't reveal my workouts. After attaching an oxygen level reading device on my finger, his eyebrows went up in surprise at the good numbers.

Gently pulling on the device's cord, he led me outside in his parking lot.

We walked, then strode, then jogged together around the lot, him still reading the device on my pointer finger. We both started laughing as people gawked at us.

"This is impossible," he said, looking at my fantastic numbers.

I had officially turned a corner on my recovery.

It was a full six months before I could even begin to feel at home in the land of the living and become "grounded" again.

100

Subtle Shifts

When my extended illness and hospital recovery period ceased, I faced a daily challenge of becoming "normal" again. I required assistance with any physical activity too taxing for debilitated muscles.

Since taking up outdoor walking during our stay at Glen's relatives, I still constantly reminded myself to keep my head up and shoulders back. My post-hospital gait and posture mirrored a feeble octogenarian's slouch.

Glen liked to remind me that he favored a woman who depended on him. Our relationship before my illness had suffered from my constant insistence on taking care of myself in everyday situations.

Moving into our new home proved taxing for me and for our relationship.

When he left in the morning for work, Glen instructed me to leave our hill of unopened moving boxes for him to unpack later. I was permitted to watch television, bathe, and feed myself. That I take at least one nap a day was another of his requirements.

I couldn't do it!

As soon as he pulled out of the driveway, I slit open a box and slowly, carefully removed one item, sat and rested a moment, and shuffled to one of our eight small rooms and placed it where it belonged.

It could take me an entire day to empty one box, but I enjoyed every minute of it. When Glen came home, he barely noticed one box less in the living room. However, as the days went by, the pile grew smaller, and even though I spread the cartons out to look like more, he discovered my deception.

"I told you to take it easy," he said, "and leave that work for me."

This small divide initiated the gradual unraveling of the marriage between two alpha dogs.

Glen and I had shared our stories of his previous three failed marriages and my two. We only agreed to try one more time after promising each other that this time was forever, no matter what. Our minimum goal, but not the primary one, was to stay together for at least ten years—longer than any of our prior relationships.

This was only a few months into our engagement period, and we had a long, long way to go.

101

Eden Mini-Tour

A couple of months following my release from the hospital, Glen shook me one morning as I groaned loudly in my sleep.

"No," I cried, "the Heaven feeling is slipping away. Let me alone!"

Equating "Heaven feeling" with my death, he shook me with more force.

Now fully conscious, I covered my eyes and mourned with deep sighs.

A vision, complete with the ecstasy of heaven, faded but remained etched in my mind. I tried to explain to Glen the unexpected visit from Ernie, who led me on a tour of an unearthly gorgeous and abundant garden.

I hadn't seen or heard from Ernie since my break up with Ray over a year ago.

However, before being awakened by Glen, Ernie and I were walking amid colorful blossoms, rejoicing at an amazing array of birds, and talking comfortably. We sat together on an intricately carved bench under an arbor festooned with fragrant climbing roses and trimmed with sparkling ribbons.

I'd hoped this experience was never-ending, but the vision began to decompose, and the ecstasy ceased. Thus, my moaning began.

Glen stared wordlessly at me as I puzzled about seeing Ernie so clearly.

Two days later, I received a call from a friend who also knew Ernie. She apologized for the news she felt compelled to share, cognizant of all I recently endured with my illness and slow recovery.

"Ernie passed away a couple of days ago," she said. "When he visited his doctor last year, expecting good news concerning his cancer, he received a death sentence. There wasn't anything more they could do."

"Since you and Ray broke up, I assumed he didn't tell you about Ernie. I'm so sorry," she concluded. "I know you two were very close and thought you deserved to know."

"I do know," I replied with a smile as the vision replayed in my mind. "Ernie came to tell me and show me his garden in Eden. God did love him after all!"

102

Close To Heaven

One beautiful morning Glen suggested we take a ride in the single-engine Piper Cherokee he kept hangered at the city airport. Before my brush with death, I'd become uneasy with any possible danger.

But with "too much left to do" still resounding in my head, I reasoned I had a long life ahead of me and wanted to relish it.

I often felt Grandma Rachael's approval for my courage and perseverance and trusted it once again.

As Glen readied the craft, I phoned my parents to tell them of our day trip to Canada via the Piper. My dad grabbed the phone from my mother when he heard the words, "Isn't that a pretty small plane for you to be in?"

"How many engines?" he barked, his mind undoubtedly racing to the memory of his own ruined plane, and him dying inside.

"One's all we need, I'm told, Dad. Besides, I'm not afraid to die anymore, and I have 'too much left to do,' so I'll be safe for a long time to come."

"What'll Glen do if the engine dies?" he continued.

"I guess we'll just float on down," I reassured him unsuccessfully.

He finished his side of the conversation with, "LIKE A TWO-TON ROCK!"

Glen and I shared an awesome day floating amongst puffy white clouds like angels. Up there, watching the boats cross the Puget Sound and being at eye level with Mt. Rainier, God felt close enough to touch.

103

Rick Continues

Rick left the planet but still stays in touch.

In addition to his many visitations via my dreams, Rick even plays tricks. After my return from the rehabilitation hospital, I unexpectedly received his wallet in the mail.

A note from Rick's widow said she thought I might like to have it. Not a scrap of anything remained in it, just the well-used wallet.

I thought it was a strange thing to send me. *Had I given the wallet to him as a gift?* I wasn't sure.

Suddenly, I remembered a secret he had told only to me a long time ago. It concerned his fear of being caught sometime without any cash.

Opening the seemingly empty wallet, I stuck my finger into a hidden slot and found the folded $50 bill he kept there in case of emergencies.

It was a gift from Rick and a reminder he still watched over me.

I still have "our" wallet.

A second strange occurrence happened shortly after Glen and I moved into our new home. It had been many years since my previous marriage, and I still preferred sleeping alone.

Since sharing the bed with my new husband, I found that his snoring prevented me from either falling asleep or staying asleep. No amount of poking turned him onto his side to solve the problem.

Sufficient sleep was mandatory for my recovery.

One restless night, I shook Glen awake and insisted that he relocate to the guest bedroom at the other end of the house. Glen, a sound sleeper, barely registered consciousness but left the room and wandered off in the direction of the guest bedroom. He left our bedroom door open as he exited, so I rose to close it, to better muffle his snores.

Not long after I returned to bed, I heard the door open, and I froze. He tiptoed to the bed, and I felt the mattress slowly sink.

With my back to him, I said sternly, "Go to the other room, please." The sneaking-into-bed process reversed, and the door was left open once more.

Angry now, I yanked off the blanket, stomped through the darkened living room toward the guest room, but hesitated when I sensed a sleeping form on the couch to my left.

The streetlight at the end of the block allowed me to find my way to him, and I leaned closer and said, "Would you please go back where you belong?" I pointed toward the guest room. The man in the shadows rose to a sitting position and appeared to stare into my face but remained silent.

I huffed back to the bedroom, closed the door, and eventually fell asleep.

The following morning, I met Glenn in the hall and asked why he was sleeping on the couch. He looked at me as if I were crazy.

"What are you talking about?" he said. "You said to go to the guest bedroom, and I did. I just now woke up."

We argued a short while about his possible sleepwalking or some other explanation, but Glen insisted he wasn't on the couch.

I was left with a strong feeling that Rick had made a Visit. The thought that I rudely sent him "back to where he belonged" caused me pain and regret. He did, however, learn to Visit me while I am sleeping.

I can differentiate a Visit from an ordinary dream.

A dream is strange and unreal, difficult to recall the next morning. It leaves me feeling unsettled.

A Visit is clear, and conversations are wonderful.

This experience brings with it a loving and profound heavenly joy. I remember every tidbit the next morning and lie in bed with a mixture of elation and sadness. The feelings stay with me throughout the day and leave me longing for heaven.

104

Slow Demise

Glen's and my initial interactions began under stressful circumstances. Each of us had recently ended serious relationships, had moved into the area from California, and were focused on heavy commitments to others.

That was the good news.

When Rick died and my health dealt me a death spiral, Glen and I were rocketed into an unforeseeable but decidedly rocky future together.

God bless Glen for getting me immediate medical attention, for seeing me through a long, distressing recovery, and never giving up on returning us to a normal life.

A year after my admittance into the first hospital, Glen and I had a small wedding and invited our family and close friends. It was a duel celebration of my survival and of my starting a new chapter of my life with Glen.

After our intimate "friends and family" wedding, we gradually proceeded to learn more about the real us. We worked well as a team in tragic circumstances, but day-to-day living proved ultimately our undoing.

We had little in common and approached life from wildly diverse backgrounds. Glen loved activities in the outdoors, and I liked to socialize with our few friends as a couple.

Glen was an identical twin, and his brother had been his "significant other" since before they were born. Realizing my second-tier status early on in our fledgling marriage left me feeling uncomfortable and vulnerable.

When dating as multi-divorced adults, we often spoke of our reluctance to marry again, but our union just seemed to materialize amidst all the health and financial struggles.

Doubts and fears about the viability of our relationship continued to plague us over the eleven years we labored to keep our vows.

Glen's work took him out of town for a supposed three-month period just weeks after we secured a new home in a small island community. We had just celebrated our fifth anniversary and bickered most of the time.

We decided to take his twin brother's advice and arrange for Glen to rent a small cabin in a State Park near the proposed job site for the summer. I would remain in our new home and settle in. Boxes of our blended belongings still stood stacked five-high in the two-car garage.

The breather would do us good, we reasoned, as Glen packed his essentials and drove north.

Somehow our prayers for "absence makes the heart grow fonder" were scrambled and we incurred "out of sight, out of mind."

Glen enjoyed his camping in the park amid the deer and elk, the friendly people he worked with, and the charming touristy town. Months passed, and Glen returned home on weekends to assist me with moving furniture and planting our half-acre homesite with flowering bushes and trees.

We enjoyed barbecuing in our scenic back yard, sipping beer, and staring at Mt. Rainier. Occasionally we joined friends for dinner, but most of Glen's time was spent with landscaping.

Instead of drawing us closer as man and wife, an easy friendship emerged. It didn't take long for Glen to begin looking forward to leaving on the weekends, and I felt happier when waving him goodbye.

The sound of the garage door opening on Friday evening now caused my stomach to tighten.

In the years Glen and I led separate lives, the space between his visits home lengthened. I only managed to drive the four-hour journey to share his cabin a handful of times. That trek necessitated battling the hectic Seattle traffic. Physically and emotionally, I wasn't up to it.

After five years of living apart, Glen was transferred back to his local office. The reintegration into each other's lives proved overwhelmingly difficult, and we sought counseling.

Phoebe, our 5'11" therapist, featured her kickboxing trophy on a shelf next to impressive degrees. She was pragmatic and cool as a cucumber, but her sense of humor tempered our serious discussions. I loved her; Glen kept both eyes on her at all times.

Our therapist's homework assignment in session three required each of us to make a list of ten positive qualities in our marriage relationship on one side and ten negative attributes on the opposite side. We were instructed to bring the list to our next session.

This tried and true assignment would, in fact, provide a crystal-clear picture of our future together.

Asked to read my list first at the next session, I did so, although my tone sounded like I was reading a book report. Truthfully, I needed to stretch to come up with ten positive things and downplayed the negatives so as not to be perceived as a bitch.

Then it was Glen's turn. Normally taciturn when speaking, Glen was a voluminous writer once his fingers hit a keyboard. He pulled approximately fifty sheets of single-spaced material from his battered briefcase and handed the tome to our speechless arbitrator.

Glancing over at Phoebe's trophy, I imagined Glen lying unconscious on the floor.

A nervous giggle escaped me as I felt the noose tightening around our marriage's throat and awaited the inevitable hanging with bated breath.

"What the hell is that?" shrieked our usually placid coach as she put up her hands in a defense position against the loose, numbered pages.

Glen looked puzzled and said, "You said to make a list, and I did." He pushed the unruly pages to her again.

I asked politely, "Glen, honey, is that the positive list or the negative list?"

Glen just glared at me as the papers began to shift and drop in ones and twos toward the floor like snowflakes.

The therapist said, "I'm not reading all that. We only have fifty minutes for the entire session. You'll just have to summarize."

I sensed that no further homework assignments would be forthcoming as Glen plopped the remaining paper to the floor, picked up his limp briefcase, and stormed out. He knew better than to slam Phoebe's door; he wasn't a fast runner.

The flustered professional woman turned to me and made my day with her final pronouncement, "I'll see you divorced from that man if it's the last thing I ever do."

105

Payback's a Bitch

As our divorce began to appear inevitable, fate threw us a curveball.

For the past decade, I'd had to force Glen to go for his annual physical. He was hale and hearty for his age, but his PSA test numbers had gradually increased over the last few years. His doctor wanted to do a biopsy to screen for cancer.

Glen and I disagreed on whether or not it was necessary. He had never been seriously sick in his life of over sixty years. He'd heard the test was very painful, so he refused to have the procedure done.

Remembering my brush with a freak, early demise, I insisted he follow the doctor's advice.

Suffice it to say, our discussions were heated, but Glen ungraciously agreed to the test if I'd share one of my stress-reducing pills with him.

On the appointed day, I drove Glen to the doctor's office and handed him a water bottle to swallow the pill. As a precaution, I took one also.

Thank heaven we had a twenty-minute wait so the pill could take effect. Glen and his family don't drink as a rule and never touch drugs. On rare occasions, it's humorous to see them stagger around and slur after one vodka-tinged coke.

A few years into our marriage, Glen caused me to belly laugh when he voiced a serious concern about my being an alcoholic. He told me he was worried because I had a glass of wine—almost every day!

Dude.

Glen was finally called into the procedure room, and it took him two full minutes to stagger down the hall, bounce off the doorframe and climb, giggling like a girl, into the stirrups on the paper-covered table.

I dozed in the reception area until Glen's tenor voice turned soprano and echoed down the hallway.

People waiting alongside me looked at one another and seemed surprised when I stifled a laugh.

Minutes later, a now very sober Glen yanked open the procedure room door and let it slam against the wall. I heard Glen's doctor reminding him to drop the file off with the receptionist as I rose to meet him at the exit.

With a flick of his hand, Glen sailed the sizable chart at the alert receptionist like a frisbee. Obviously used to such patient reactions, she ducked in time.

As I opened the door for him, Glen paused and hissed, "I'll get you for this." Then he pushed past me and carefully made his way down the hallway with a slight limp.

With all eyes on me, I waved to the people in the waiting room and told the receptionist to have a nice day.

She replied, "Don't forget to breathe," and stooped to retrieve Glen's paperwork.

106

Rubber Meets The Road

There were several times when I considered strangling Glen with my bare hands, but I wouldn't let my husband die of cancer.

Glen received a call from the doctor two days after the prostate screening and phoned me right away at home. He was chuckling when he began reporting their conversation, so I figured the test results were negative.

"The doctor said he took ten biopsies and seven of them showed cancer," he said with another chuckle.

"What?" I interrupted. "Why are you laughing?"

"You were right!" was his explanation. "It's an aggressive form. They have to operate. If we hadn't discovered it now, the doctor said I'd been dead in two years."

"See ya for dinner," he concluded.

I'd be having a glass of wine for sure.

107

Post-OP

We weathered the operation, the hospital stay, and the home recovery. Helping your spouse maneuver a catheter and urine bag into the bathroom at midnight earns you credit somewhere.

Glen was courageous and pathetic at the same time. My heart went out to him as reruns of his grace-filled care of me in two hospitals, and at our home, kept me focused on his comfort. Our marriage had called a truce.

"Why is life so darned complicated?" I asked whoever might be looking out for me in heaven at that moment. They answered right away.

"Good job," whispered Rick. "Haven't lost your touch."

"Proud of you!" Grandma Rachael cackled. "It'll get better."

I closed my eyes and breathed.

108

Lauren

I would not have survived Acute Respiratory Distress Syndrome if my daughter, Lauren, hadn't found an ARDS website with information crucial to my pulmonologist's treatment of me.

After Glen and I were wed, Lauren and her husband, Randy, moved within a block of us on the island. For the first few months, she and I spent hours a day decorating their new home and taking walks with my grand-dog, Sammy.

My daughter was my best friend, and I loved every moment we shared during their brief stay in our neighborhood. Prior to this location, they had moved often to mostly far-away places.

During the extreme financial downturn after the turn of the century, Lauren and her husband lost their home, their cars, and all but the barest of possessions. Both of their employments entailed sales and commissions, which quickly dried up.

Lauren became ill with a mysterious malady that baffled her doctors. Her physical and emotional health declined dramatically.

The stress of their financial demise caused a decline in our relationships. Harsh words were exchanged between the four of us, and feelings irreparably damaged.

They moved from the United States for a secure employment opportunity and left us with no forwarding information. It was as if they both died, but we dared not mourn, keeping hope as a distant option.

I believe Lauren checks in with her brother via email now and then, but Chris has loyally agreed not to share their electronic exchanges for fear she will disappear from his life too. Not a day goes by when I don't feel intense sorrow at her loss.

After their disappearance, I received one brief note from Lauren indicating we needed to live our lives apart. She added a promise to meet in heaven someday where we could be together, loving each other like we used to.

Clinging desperately to that probability, I continue to "wrap her in angels."

109

Gone But Not Forgotten

With Glen's return to health, the cushion of our joint project for his survival no longer aided us.

Our multiple experiences with the legalities of divorce saved us time and money. We strove to stay on a financial track instead of an emotional one. It didn't always work, but luckily when one of us got revved up, the other pushed gently but firmly on the brake.

The judge complimented us on our decorum after the divorce proceedings, and we walked back to our separate cars while holding hands.

It was genuinely nice to be friends again, and we've stayed close ever since. His new fiancée and my significant other are often puzzled by our relationship, but we did save each other's lives, and that counts for a lot.

110

My People

During my lengthy recovery, I devoured every book I could find relating to people who died and "came back."

I learned of the term "near-death experience," also known as an NDE, and found numerous stories of people rejoicing in heavenly ecstasies. They glowed in other-worldly lights and excitedly conversed with Jesus on heavenly ocean shores. These lucky ones met with deceased loved ones, interacted with angels, and even talked with God.

I found little information on the "Dark NDEs," like the one I experienced. When I located a story of one, it oddly brought me comfort. I wasn't alone in my journey through hell after all. However, no one explained in writing why they went this dismal direction.

My Descent Into Death by Howard Storm, a difficult read for the uninitiated, caused me to rejoice! I found multiple similarities in his hell depiction and his stressful recovery. He talked to Jesus, for heaven's sake! I felt robbed, but also felt part of a select and special group. I was once more "the new kid," but this time, it was better late than never.

I appreciated *Blessing in Disguise* by Barbara R. Rommer, M.D. and *The Uttermost Deep* by Gracia Fay Ellwood. *Dancing Past the Darkness* and *The Buddha in Hell* by Nancy Evans Bush gave me context and a safe place to explore. Their experiences and what they extrapolated from them brushed up against mine but didn't hit the target on my deepest issues.

I continued to write and rewrite my experiences. Although endeavoring to fine-tune the descriptions, I didn't dig deeper into the meaning of it all. As the years passed, the abject terror of hell diminished with the grounding of day-to-day human living.

Still, I hungered for explanations, lessons learned, and guidelines for my future. *What the devil was that experience about?*

Gradually, I gathered the courage to expose my greatest fears. As I sat quietly in an empty church years after the life-altering events, I asked God direct questions.

"Why did I go to hell? I really wasn't that bad, was I? How do I keep from ending up there again?"

The faithful Voice's litany calmed me. "It's all in the plan. You'll figure it out. I'm here; have faith. You are never alone." I clung to these simple phrases and repeated them each time I felt the darkness approach me. I continued to pray for clarity.

After many years, through an incredible chain of serendipitous happenings, I found my way to the International Association of Near-

Death Studies, aka IANDS, in Seattle, WA. I had promised a friend of a friend, who I met at a meeting I had not wanted to attend, that I would contact Todd at IANDS. She had pressed a paper with his phone number into my hand.

Just before Christmas, as my third marriage fell apart, and I was feeling abject misery over the loss of my daughter, my will to live faltered. I scrounged around to locate the piece of paper with the IANDS number on it.

Doubting a positive outcome, but at the end of my rope, I called Todd. He listened patiently as I shared my horrible hell experience with great detail, my brief heaven visit with Rick, and my interaction with the ladies by the stream.

At the conclusion of the epic tale, I was a blubbering mess. The tissues piled up on both sides of me as I crouched in the chair like a frightened child.

After asking me a multitude of IANDS standard questions to authenticate my experience, Todd pronounced it "valid"; as valid as all the experiences I had been reading about in the NDE books.

Todd informed me that the Dark NDE I had experienced only occurred about 20 percent of the time. Experts weren't sure if the Dark ones really happened less often or if the Dark NDE experiencers were reluctant to report them. The latter seemed a likely scenario to me.

Who likes to share being gang-raped by AIDS-ridden zombies?

111

Soul Searching

Todd peppered me with additional uncomfortable questions as I feebly attempted to escape from the buzzing of demons in my tortured memories. My quickening breath included soft moans.

"Do you blame yourself for ending up in hell?" he wondered aloud dispassionately. "What did you do in your lifetime to deserve it? Weren't you a Catholic? Are you still?"

These questions had already haunted me for over a decade, and the answers I'd managed to stitch together seemed half-hearted and as nebulous as storm clouds.

As I began to lose my composure, Todd didn't seem to mind or to care. He was used to it, having heard hundreds of NDEs. Even joyful, loving experiences contort our emotions. It's typical for most experiencers to mourn extensively after returning to Earth, whether willingly or unwillingly.

I continued to pine like a love-struck teen as a result of my bum's rush from Paradise and the demotion to heaven expatriate. The indescribable longing for an eternity with God and my beloved Rick ached in my soul like a festering tooth.

"Just start talking," encouraged Todd with a tinge of impatience. "Let it out."

Angry from Todd's painful prodding, anger at a supposedly all-loving God, and the fury with my unholy self whirled into a tornado of hateful and destructive words.

"God damn it, Todd! I don't understand the whole crappy scenario either!" I shouted. "You are the first living soul ever to hear my whole hideous story. This regurgitation in minute detail is pushing me eyeball to eyeball with the dark despair I have barely kept at bay for over ten years."

Resisting the overwhelming urge to disconnect the call and return to my imaginary safety, I grabbed at my tissue box and swiped with vigor at my hot tears.

Todd's calm voice invited me "to breathe." I barely resisted retorting with a phrase starting with an "f" and ending with "you."

Instead, I attempted to end our conversation with a promise to contemplate his intrusive questions and get back to him sometime in the far-distant future, but he persisted.

112

Healing Commences

Todd begged me to come to an upcoming IANDS monthly meeting in Seattle and share my complex experience with the large group. He said the IANDS members, and additional visitors to the monthly meetings, would benefit from my unusual perspective.

I just gave him a sarcastic laugh and sternly said, “No!”

In telling Todd my story, a mixture of relief, embarrassment, and flashback anxiety had forced me into a second box of tissues. Trembling in my chair, I could barely speak.

What would happen to me in front of a crowd of strangers? This new kid in the club wasn’t up to it, I explained.

Todd made me promise to call him back after Christmas, and when I didn’t, he made the call to me. After offering an invitation just to attend the next meeting, he assured me I could get a feel for the membership and hear other NDEers tell their stories.

It took many months, but finally my Voice made me go.

113

The Voice

My experience with the Voice began as a youngster, and it converses with me in my mind when I am praying. It seems to emanate from God, my conscience, or a guardian angel, depending on the circumstances. We all have the ability to hear the Voice, I believe, but one has to be open to it.

Since my return from "the other side," the Voice seems to converse with me on its own terms. I don't need to sit quietly in church and await it; it speaks right up.

The morning of my first IANDS meeting, I decided not to go. The Voice told me to get in the car. I continued to argue with the Voice as I drove north. An hour later, I found myself in a meeting room surrounded by all types, sizes, and ages of people.

It was mildly interesting, but I did not feel connected. I can't remember the speaker's name, but her NDE was wonderful and full of joy and angels and blah, blah, blah. I didn't fit in.

Months later, an IANDS email reminded me that a famous neurosurgeon would be the featured speaker that afternoon. He sounded interesting, but I didn't really want to drive that far. However, the Voice insisted, "You need to meet a special person there and you must attend."

Drat. I got my car keys.

I had viewed this Voice skeptically the first time I heard it in my head and half-believed it to be a figment of my imagination. I told myself it was definitely time to test my Voice once and for all.

Determined to make it difficult for the Voice's prediction to come to pass, I'd leave no wiggle room to determine its trustworthiness.

Arriving intentionally early at the unfamiliar location, I was startled at the size of the auditorium and the immense number of chairs, nearly all of them empty now. My prior experience of an IANDS gathering took place in a small room at the back of a library, with an audience of maybe sixty.

Preparing to test the Voice on my supposed need to meet a "special person," I looked toward a large vacant area, walked down the aisle in the middle of it, and sat in an end chair to better see the speaker.

I counted seven empty rows in front of me and seven behind. To my right was a row of ten or more empty chairs. I waited, avoiding eye contact so as not to encourage someone to sit next to me.

Within ten minutes, my peripheral vision noticed a young woman walking slowly down the aisle at the far end of my row. I looked down at some brochures in my lap.

Appearing to be scouting out a good seat, she suddenly halted and cocked her head slightly. Backing up without turning around, she entered my row, walked past all the empty chairs, sat right next to me, and said, "Hi!"

It was fortunate I was already sitting down because I was flabbergasted. She looked around, waved at various acquaintances, then proceeded to study the program.

After a few minutes, she asked if I had heard the speaker before, if I was new to IANDS, and other innocuous questions. I answered succinctly but was still shaken and a little anxious. She appeared to be younger and thinner than I was and dressed in casual but colorful clothing.

Finally, the speaker was introduced and commenced with his NDE. I could not believe my ears as he told of his background, education, and finally, his death. I hung on every word, amazed at his intelligence, professional experience, and ease with which he shared his truth.

Wow, I'm sure glad I decided to come to this presentation!

The Voice probably rolled Its eyes if It had any.

At the break, full of excitement and wonder, I turned to the mystery lady and fully expected to shock her with, "I was supposed to meet you here today!"

She didn't hesitate, only flashed a conspiratorial smile and calmly answered, "I know."

This was too much. I asked her, "How did you know?"

She smiled. "I was walking down the aisle, wondering where to sit, when my Voice told me, 'Go sit by that lady; she's very nice.'"

I grabbed her forearm and asked, "Your Voice?"

"Sure," she said. "Don't you hear it?"

I nodded with my mouth agape.

"Don't worry. You'll get used to it," she said as she turned to hear the speaker resume his spellbinding tale. "By the way," she said, "my name's Adele. I died in New Orleans."

Another incident involving this enhanced ability occurred after I was called over by Todd at the intermission of another meeting.

He introduced me to a frightened young man named Paul. An air of homelessness clung to him. He had come to this meeting to seek understanding and support over a "bad vision" that had haunted him since childhood.

His darting eyes reminded me of a frightened deer as he attempted to make himself small in the crowded room.

Todd filled me in by paraphrasing Paul's story. The few IANDS meetings Paul attended so far featured heavenly NDEs, and they only made him feel more isolated and negative about himself.

I agreed to talk with Paul after the meeting to give him a synopsis of my dark story. Paul timidly shared his frightening experience with me and added his hearing mine offered comfort and hope. We agreed to hang out at meetings together in the future.

Coincidentally, Paul also became particularly good friends with Adele.

As time went on, Paul shared with me his service to the poor at a local church and his budding career as a writer. He was living with friends and still had issues but didn't dwell on his distressful experience anymore.

I ceased attending meetings one winter because of poor driving conditions. Finally, spring arrived and on a warm, clear day I decided to attend a meeting at the last minute. I sent a text to my young friend, Paul, asking him to save me a seat at the meeting. When I arrived late, I searched the crowd but didn't spot him, so I sat in the back row.

A few minutes later, I spied Paul scanning the room from the doorway. When he saw me and waved, I gestured for him to join me. As he sat down, Paul whispered, "Thanks for saving me a seat."

"You were supposed to save me one," I whispered as the speaker was announced. He looked at me strangely.

I reminded him, "I texted you earlier and asked you to do that." Paul was a guileless young man who did not have much of a sense of humor, so I took his next remark as truth.

Looking into my eyes, Paul said, “I left my phone at home this morning and was just wandering around town ‘til now. I didn’t receive your text. My Voice told me you’d save me a seat, so I came to the meeting.”

Hmm, this stuff is starting to feel normal.

114

Unfinished Business

The two "living people" I interacted with in hell needed to be warned against future problems. My dilemma was: how would I approach them?

I considered, "Say, I saw you in hell recently, and you need to change your ways, or there'll be hell to pay," then took some time to formulate a better approach. Needless to say, neither interaction was well received.

The first person, observed in the faux beauty parlor, exhibited insult at my tale-telling, and within a few years, wrote me out of her life. I hear from our friends that her continued attempts at fighting the effects of aging consume her thoughts and income.

The young woman observed at the dinner party initially blew off the incident, until recently. Twenty years later, she wanted to hear the warning again.

The lavish dinner I witnessed in hell, and what it represented, actually occurred. The effects of a crippling relationship, and eventual horrific break-up, led her to an eating disorder.

Her husband treated her as a second-class citizen and used her talents as a wonderful cook to entertain the senior staff of his company to further his career goals. His eventual cheating on her and habitual lying brought her to the brink of despair.

As I shared my vision of her in hell for this second time, she interjected explanations for the scene I had described to her long ago. Her lingering feelings of guilt over the marital breakup dissolved, and relief and gratitude bolstered her future.

Her new husband is a wonderful role model for her children and encouraged her to start her own successful business. I am so happy for her and wish my vision had benefited her earlier.

115

Meeting Matthew

Many years after my near-death experience, and just before attending an NDE conference, I spent an evening searching for some old pictures my mother asked me to find. I kept them with miscellaneous items in two large plastic boxes under the bed in my spare bedroom.

After dragging the two boxes from their hidey-hole, I proceeded to take out handfuls of memorabilia, pause and reflect on their importance, and proceed to the next bunch.

Wedding pictures from each of my marriages prompted "what if" moments as I searched. My varied photographed expressions told stories, and a mixture of emotional memories flooded in.

Multiple photographs of jubilant times with Rick caused me feelings of joy and great loss. I needed my box of tissues to finish the search.

A couple of weeks later, during a break at the NDE convention, I visited a room filled with author's books for sale, psychics offering readings, and where spiritual amulets for sale abounded.

One psychic claimed to offer clients conversations with deceased loved ones. The offer struck a chord, and I paused at her empty table.

A desire to communicate with Kathleen overwhelmed me, and I signed up for a reading later in the afternoon.

At the appointed hour, I vowed not to offer much personal information to the untried seer to force her to intuit rather than guess. When prompted, I told her I desired to speak to my daughter.

The middle-aged lady, who appeared quite average, closed her eyes and folded her hands. She abruptly declared no daughter available, but my young, blond son wished to speak to me.

Recoiling, my heart raced as I mentally sought an explanation.

"I don't have a dead son," I blurted, although my face flushed in shame.

With her eyes closed, she began again. "He says he only wanted to be in human form for a short time and chose to be part of your life before coming to Earth."

"I don't believe this," I sputtered. "Give me some proof."

Immediately came a reply, "Tell her she recently sat looking at pictures and wondering, *What if?*"

"No, that can't be," I retorted, my mind filling with the memory of the murderous coil and the bloody consequence.

The psychic grabbed a small, blank piece of paper and picked up a loose pencil. She began drawing and said frantically, "He says you are always drawing hearts."

"What are you talking about?" I said in a voice louder than I intended, and tears filled my eyes.

She turned the paper to face me, and I gasped at the sight of the two small, offset hearts touching at the curving lines. The same hearts I always add to my greeting cards and their envelopes.

I managed to calm my voice enough to say, "I'm so very sorry" to my unborn son, then grabbed a tissue from the side of the woman's folding table.

She reached out and put her hand over mine.

"He really hopes you can understand and accept his choice to be in your life in that way. His spirit always stays at your side, and he loves you deeply."

My fifteen-minute session expired, and the woman stood to gently dismiss me as a man moved eagerly toward my chair.

The shock and awe of the revelation required time and introspection to assimilate. Shortly after our formal introduction, I claimed my spiritual son and named him Matthew, the alternative name I chose for my first baby, had Kathleen been born a boy.

Matthew doesn't require a plot or a memorial stone; he and I are inseparable for the remainder of my life.

116

Junior's Redemption

My younger brother's descent into a living hell was a long, slow one. Junior managed to engage in normal activities as a functioning alcoholic for many years. During this time, he married a sweet woman whose parents were also alcoholics. Junior's proclivities looked normal to her.

As their children grew, his disease progressed. He stayed at the bar too long after work one night and almost died in an automobile accident. The firemen used the Jaws of Life to pull him out of his totaled car at the bottom of a ditch, but his body still housed his blacked-out mind.

Our family fought to retain some semblance of hope as he endured two tours in alcohol rehabilitation centers over a five-year period. Both were sponsored by his employers, who valued him as their best worker when sober.

Everybody loved Junior, except when he put a drink in his mouth. One could sense the self-loathing he felt, and the resulting destructive behavior pushed his family and admirers away from him.

Junior attended countless Alcoholics Anonymous meetings and managed months of sobriety on multiple occasions. At these awesome times in his life, the magnetism of his cheerful disposition and witty humor drew us all back to him.

He became a sponsor to others suffering his disease and became a favorite with the younger addicts. We would only know the blessing of his sufferings at his upcoming funeral.

Falling off the wagon once too often, and at risk of losing his job, his long-suffering wife divorced him, but Junior's beloved children continued to give him one more chance after another until they ran out.

I attended family sessions at his rehabilitation attempts on many occasions and often wondered why fate prompted me to add the X's to Mom's calendar so long ago.

Near the end, I visited a buzzed Junior in his cramped, dingy apartment and cried as I gave him a hug goodbye. My heart broke knowing I'd probably never see him again.

He whispered, "I love you, sis. I'm so very tired, and the family keeps rescuing me. I'm going to kill myself and get out of this hell once and for all."

I held him at arm's length, observing his long, dirty hair and hopeless eyes and advised him against taking his own life.

With a short explanation of my experience in hell and heaven, in addition to my learning of negative happenings from suicidal people who returned, I offered an alternative solution.

"The next time you feel your death approaching, find a safe spot to stay with a friend, tell them to let you sleep undisturbed, and let yourself go."

A week later, he did just that.

Although my family mourned his passing without saving him one more time, I sent a prayer of thanksgiving for the peace and love he now enjoyed.

We held a memorial service and chose the smallest room in which to celebrate. Counting only on the attendance of family and a few of his former workmates and friends, I arrived minutes before the service commenced after finally finding a parking space down the street.

The room, filled to overflowing and full of noisy conversations, caused me to double-check the name posted at the door. It was Junior's room all right.

Standing on my toes, I spied my family in the front row and the empty seat reserved for me. Making my way through the crowded aisle, I slipped into my chair and smiled into the surprised faces of my parents and sister.

As our priest took the podium, he beamed at the crowd and joked about Junior always loving a good party. Having known our family for many years, the sermon was light and evoked laughter as he recalled Junior's life and adventures.

To our family's surprise, Junior's long war with alcohol, and then drugs, resulted in his service to many in his role as a sponsor.

My sister spoke for our family and gave an upbeat eulogy, which received applause instead of tears. She and Junior were amazingly close throughout their lives, and her mothering of him through his bouts of destruction and despair was one of her life's dedications.

When the priest asked if others wished to say something about Junior, a lengthy line formed at the podium.

Our family sat dumbfounded, and grateful, as one young person after another spoke of Junior's *saving their life*. Each story of Junior's good-hearted, patient listening to these kids as they struggled in the rehab centers or at Alcoholics Anonymous captivated us.

Junior had repeatedly rescued this crowd of young people from using drugs or alcohol, drove them home, sobered them up, and in general, gave them a personal understanding of their problems with his own life of destructive behavior.

There wasn't a dry eye in the house as weeping teenagers praised our lost loved one with gratitude and honor.

After the service and the sharing of a prepared luncheon for all attending, my mother put her arm through mine and chuckled. "Were all those kids sure it was Junior?"

My sister couldn't forgive herself for not saving him this last time but called me a few days later with unexpected joy in her voice.

"I saw him!" she began. "I was driving to the store and came to a stop sign. A tall hedge was on my right, and my eyes noticed a sudden movement there. A man seemed to come out of the hedge, ran in front of my car, and stopped at my open window."

"Hi, sis," he said.

I recognized him, although he looked a lot younger and healthy, too.

"Junior?" I asked him in shock.

The young man kept out of reach but continued, "Just wanted you to know I'm OK; in fact, I'm great! No need to worry about me anymore. Gotta go! Love ya!"

With that, he darted in front of the car and disappeared into the hedge.

"He's in heaven," Lynn said with tears in her voice. "He's finally happy and at peace."

117

Lynn

The middle child of our family, Lynn, is the peacemaker and nurturer. Without an ounce of guile, she is often wounded by those taking advantage of her good heart.

Anyone who knows her loves and respects her, even though the quirkiness of many generations seems to have percolated through the genes and infused her with a plethora of endearing hiccups.

Although squishy with feelings, Lynn's been my rock.

Months after my Dark NDE experience, I had attempted to convince Lynn of the reality of hell and the awaiting punishment for our sins.

Born again in her forties, and still Jesus' number one fan, she scoffed at my warnings and told me, "Don't know what happened in your case, sis, but when I die, I'm jetting right into Jesus' arms."

I sighed and said, "Don't count on it, my dear. Better consider a Plan B."

"Nope, I'm good," remained her final answer.

During the long months of my mental, spiritual, and physical recuperation, I frequently recalled her joyful vehemence and desired with all my soul to have her confidence.

118

A Missionary to Hell

At an IANDS meeting a year after joining the organization, my friend Adele asked if I was going to tell my story to the group. She immediately confided her reluctance to share hers.

We had talked briefly to each other of our experiences in private, but us speaking publicly seemed highly unlikely.

Todd was pushing for us to share our stories, and Adele had an idea to make it possible. She offered to sit in the center seat of the front row while I told my story onstage. I could speak directly to Adele, concentrating only on her face and pretending no one else was there.

If I was brave enough to follow her plan, Adele agreed to do likewise with her story, only looking at me. It seemed so crazy it just might work. I agreed to be the featured speaker at the next meeting.

God not only works in strange ways, but if we cooperate, we can get a pleasant surprise sometimes. After the first few minutes of fidgeting in my chair while facing a packed house, my love of storytelling kicked in, and I was off and running, glancing at my friend only now and then.

The audience was rapt as they traversed my journey through hell. We shared the terror, and the near despair, and after we sang our Christmas carol into heaven, the applause was loud and long. How utterly amazing!

A sea of hands went up when I asked if there were any questions. Some answers were easy to give, but most were involved. When the dreaded question, "Why do you think you were sent to hell?" was asked, the room fell silent and all eyes riveted on me. Looking down at my front-row friend didn't help.

From the audience, Todd lifted his voice, "She was a missionary to hell."

I felt surprised when that phrase struck a chord deep inside me, something about being a missionary to Tanoshi and the Japanese. Mentally sidetracked, I asked him to repeat his explanation.

Todd smiled broadly and confidently repeated his answer, "You were a missionary to hell, sent there to tell those souls they didn't have to do horrible things and that they shouldn't despair."

For the first time since my untimely death, I felt a shred of vindication. Better yet, God's working in strange ways seemed to deserve a second look. This dim enlightenment allowed me to see something boarding on positive in that ungodly damnation trip.

With this fresh perspective, I felt emboldened to take another look at my NDE.

119

Dissipating Fog

What if... I asked myself that evening as I lay in bed. A myriad of questions beginning with those two small words threatened to open a humongous can of writhing worms. Any thoughts of a restful night's sleep evaporated.

What if I created my own hell and wrote my own ticket to dwell there?

What if my childhood indoctrinations were skewed, incorrect, or downright lies?

What if, what if, what if?

Recaps of horrendous events in my life assaulted me like lightning flashes of memories: the death of my infant, rape, the inability to give my children a stable homelife, constant upheaval in my personal relationships, my ongoing disappointment with God's inaction at times of distress.

Innumerable snapshots of despair caused me to cry out to the universe, "STOP!"

I threw off my covers and double-timed to my computer to drag the detritus from my mind and spew it onto paper.

Although I wrote all night, and knew I was on to something tremendously important, fear and dread hung over my weary shoulders and drooled on my soul.

120

Reality, Logic, or Something Else?

With high SAT scores in logic and math, I started with the basic facts; what I deemed reliable. *My whole life might only be a trick question*, I reasoned.

In heaven, I, and countless others, experienced God as pure love. Since God is only pure love, it's impossible to *make* God unhappy, jealous, or angry.

God will always be merciful and forgiving; therefore, the only person to judge me is myself. This self-judgement is attested to by hundreds of NDE experiencers in their sharing of personal "life reviews."

I believe our "image and likeness" to God is our divine soul, not our human bodies, and I believe He gave us free will.

Up to the time of my NDE, I believed I'd go to purgatory, aka hell, by committing a sinful act of omission or commission, via the use of my free will, with the implied agreement to accept the "penance/consequence" equivalent to those sins.

Thus, I needed to create my own section in hell in which to experience the consequence.

For example, if I ate meat on Friday, in the time when my church proclaimed it a sin to eat meat, and accepted I would pay a fine for eating it that day, then I did indeed incur a penalty.

However, again at my church's proclamation, if I said certain prayers, or performed specific good actions, I would earn indulgences/credits to the tune of 300 days, or some such discernible amount, off my purgatory sentence.

It came down to mathematics, and most Catholic kids became particularly good at this form of math.

Fifty-three years of my life as a human being made for a lot of numerical calculations, and I obviously misjudged the totals in the plus and minus columns. My years of human bookkeeping experience somehow had not served me well in this spiritual arena.

So, having accepted the agreement to go to purgatory, and even though I had conveniently pushed that particular deal out of my consciousness after my sin cooled down, it wasn't God, but myself, who damned me.

The bottom line on this rational formula wasn't very appealing, but worth pursuing further.

121

Breathe

Never do I want to experience purgatory again, and I absolutely freak at the thought of my loved ones experiencing hell.

I do consider that some people may choose hell by default because they hate God and love evil. If they want no part of God, they achieve their objective by choosing hell. It's not for me to judge anyone, but this seems logical yet extraordinarily tragic.

As I dissected the tragedies of my life, especially the experiences that I've depicted as hellish, I reflected on possible corollaries in my actual hell scenarios. I experienced shock at the many parallels.

Recalling my fear and guilt at darting a young man to near death, the nagging implication that I murdered my helpless infant by signing a form ordering her removal from life support, and the use of the coil to abort a mini-Matthew caused the vision of the abortion clinic in hell to jump up and shout "BOO!"

The gang rape scene in the other world caused me to shudder as it induced feelings of vulnerability and despair wrestling with the peace officer.

I sensed a theme but drew no conclusions.

How could any of this help others? I thought. An overwhelming sadness welled up inside me. I felt powerless and insignificant.

My Voice answered, “Breathe.”

122

No Good Deed Goes Unpunished

I came to appreciate the unwritten rule of the universe fully, "No good deed goes unpunished," after years of dismissing it as a harmless, negative play on words.

My beliefs have always included the acceptance of evil lurking in our lives. Since my foray into evil's realm, however, I learned first-hand that evil is jealous, mean, resentful, and relentless.

Should a person go an extra mile to bring love and kindness into another's life, evil seeks a way to retaliate, to rebalance the scales.

A prime example in my life of such punishment resulted from a simple act of kindness, which occurred several years after my NDE.

An introduction to a handsome couple at a luncheon left me puzzled at their disproportionate physiques. Bob stood all of 6'4", and obviously spent a lot of time at the gym. In contrast, his gentrified, petite wife, Tina, stretched to 5'4" in heels, and lifted teacups.

A few days later, a fellow I was newly dating reintroduced me to the same couple at his favorite veteran's bar hangout one evening. Tina still appeared the same, but Bob looked like a giant-sized, unsavory lady of the evening.

I said, "Hi," and smiled weakly as my date chatted with them for a few minutes.

I wondered if this was a Halloween get-together. After all, it was late October. My date showed me to a table where his friends saved us seats. I perused the crowded bar for others in costume as we settled in next to the band's stage and small dance floor.

After introducing me to his friends at the table, and noting the confusion on my face, my companion shared the story behind the man's appearance.

Our subject presented himself as a handsome, cultured gentleman by day, but Bob spent his evenings singing in a Country-Western honky-tonk as Gunsmoke's Miss Kitty. His controversial double life offered an outlet for coping with severe post-traumatic stress incurred in multiple tours of hell in the Vietnam War.

Bob's beautiful wife, and wizened veteran buddies, lovingly accepted his playing dress up and respected his attempt to balance a shattered psyche.

Remembering my own personal rejections as a scrawny, crippled social discard during my illness, I vowed to heap kindness on them instead of reacting with the same judgment that caused my own soul to wither.

Over many months, when my new circle of friends met for two-stepping and cold beers, I'd strike up an occasional conversation with the seemingly mismatched pair as they sat at the bar. We soon joked with one another and became friends.

When the music fired up, "Miss Kitty" would slink (as well as a hulking giant in five-inch high heels could) to the microphone and dazzle us with heart-breaking slow songs and shit-kicking fast numbers with a perfect-tenor voice.

Kitty's outfit sparkled and spangled from the leather bustier to the black fishnets, evoking a barrage of comments from newcomers, unused to such a peculiar entertainer.

The local fellas, and the Vietnam-hatted veterans, quickly quelled any serious attempt to disturb their local star and remained loyal and vigilant.

One night, on an adventuresome whim, I asked Kitty/Bob to dance as a slow instrumental number started up. We waved our arms comically up and down, trying to decide who was to lead.

Other dancers laughed with us as he declared in his gruff day-time voice, and evening short skirt, "Hey, I get to lead. I'm the man."

At about 6'8" in his stilettos, and me at 5'2", I stared at eye level with his oversized boobs as we danced. I began belly laughing as the foam rubber cups pressed into my face, and I prayed I wouldn't dampen my undies in the process.

Without much thought, I paused, still holding on to him with one hand, stood on an empty chair, and hopped atop a table. Surprised, he looked up at me, drew me closer, and began swaying me back and forth as if we were still dancing. His head lay on my shoulder.

At the end of the song, people started clapping, and we took our bows. Faux Kitty looked into my eyes, arms still around me, and sniffed back an awkward tear.

"This is the first hug I've ever had from someone taller than me, even as a little kid."

Shocked by his painful sharing, I dropped his hand, intending to step back onto the chair, then descend to the floor so I could continue our conversation.

Disaster struck as the aforementioned Law of the Universe retaliated.

The chair's rollers seemed possessed as they retracted beneath the table with my first step, and I was flung forward across the concrete floor, landing on my left side. From head to toe, I smacked the surface with my entire length, with nothing to protect, or deflect, injury from my body.

My next conscious thought occurred as I stared up at a crowd of my friends, surrounding me as I lay flat on my back.

Two or three of them remarked how glad they were that I finally awoke. One suggested calling an ambulance.

I fought the idea and insisted no unconsciousness had occurred, but the feedback was swift and sure. The normally rough and tumble crowd appeared docile and pensive.

Fear filled me concerning damage to my back, since only eight months prior to this accident, I endured a spinal fusion, and my surgeon didn't condone diving off tables.

"SHIT!" seemed an appropriate epitaph as I attempted to rise from the floor, which required several awkward attempts. Feeling completely humiliated, nauseous, and concerned for my injured back, I snatched my purse from a friend and bade them all good evening.

Bob, white-faced despite the garish make-up, insisted on walking me to my car after my refusal of his offer for a ride home. Attempting to keep up with me as I zigzagged down the hallway, his ankles wobbled in the ridiculously high heels.

I asked too gruffly, "How in the hell do you walk in those damn things?"

"Lots of practice, I guess," was the innocent reply.

Holding the door ajar, he made sure I made it safely to my vehicle.

I never saw Kitty or his wife again.

The result of my concussion was severe double-vision, which made it difficult to drive, watch television, or read. I also found it distracting to converse with two-headed people.

I suffered two years with this debilitating condition. With no reversal to normal sight likely, per the four eye specialists I consulted, I almost stopped praying for a miracle.

My final optometrist charged an arm and a leg for an in-depth series of tests and formulated a prescription incorporating prisms into a pair of awfully expensive glasses.

Calling in all favors from deceased friends and relatives for prayers, I donned the promising glasses and looked hopefully at the eye chart. Like magic, my doubled vision wobbled, then coalesced into one perfect line.

I wept with gratitude then but now offer a prayer of thanksgiving every time I place the two precious pieces of glass to my face, rejoicing in the restored gift of sight.

My acts of kindness to Bob and his wife were still worth the consequences.

123

First Aha! Moment

On a routine trip to California to visit my family, I experienced a 6.8 rolling earthquake on my shuttle bus ride to the Seattle airport. When the driver eyed the intact terminal, he dropped us at the entrance, where I noted crowds of people milling about on their phones and many others sitting on the curbs smoking.

Inside, distressed would-be passengers formed unending, ragged lines to the ticket counters. I heard employees shout, "Computers are still out! All flights are canceled! Stay out of the underground trains!"

Taking stock, I patted my carry-on bag and felt reassured by my pre-packed lunch but cursed my last-minute decision not to add a bottle of water. I found the end of my airline ticket line about a block away behind the restaurants.

Fifty-nine minutes later, a frazzled agent accepted my two bags, handed me receipts, then told me the flight was delayed four to five hours, if I was lucky. She added, "Better stay in the main area. Emergency crews are evacuating the injured now."

Shouldering my way to a kiosk stand to purchase a bottle of water, I found a locked screen over the entry and a cardboard sign proclaiming, "Out of bottled water. Fountains aren't working either. Good luck!"

I remembered a small bar I'd passed while creeping through the line and pushed through the crowd like a salmon going upstream in low tide.

Standing on tiptoe, I spied a lone stool next to a guy wearing a weathered Stetson and cowboy boots. Dragging my carry-on as quickly as possible through the sea of bodies, I asked him, "This seat taken?"

Slowly turning his attention away from his beer, obviously not his first of the day, he eyed me up and down, tipped his hat, and said with a drawl, "Just savin' it for you, darlin'."

Swell, I thought, but sat down quickly, tucking my bag between my knees. *My luck just keeps getting better and better.*

The bartender lifted his voice above the din and shouted: *$6 beers are now $20, and we're running out! Cash only!*

$20 was the sum total of my traveling money, but I broke a nail digging into my purse, fishing for my wallet.

The cowboy held up his hand. "Let me do a good deed, miss. Barkeep! The best beer for my girl here, and three extras." Then he introduced himself as Tex.

Surprised by his gentle and generous offer, I smiled and said, "Thanks, Tex. I'm Rachael."

With hours to kill and the beers he'd purchased, we discussed the earthquake, took a bet on whether or not we'd fly out that day, shared our destinations, and then eased into more personal topics.

"What's a nice gal like you doin' in Seattle, for crying out loud?" he said.

I observed his tall, lanky frame drooping loosely over the bar and pale blue eyes underlined with sadness. His beard, streaked with grey, sprung from his weathered face, and even his apparel appeared dispirited.

Easing into my painful story, I shared an abridged version of Rick's illness, my attempt at keeping him alive, and the tragic loss at his death.

Tex sat with full attention as I moved on to my illness, told him the good part of my near-death experience, and he gasped when I told him of seeing Rick in heaven.

Needing to shift the focus from myself, I asked if his wife was awaiting his return home.

Tex winced and took a long pull on his warm beer. His voice cracked when he said, "She died of a freak heart attack in '98."

"I'm so sorry!" I blurted and placed my hand lightly on his forearm.

He shook his head. "I don't know why I told you that. I never talk to anyone 'bout it."

His tear-filled eyes sought mine. He was the oldest young man I'd ever seen.

As the story poured out, he picked up a staccato rhythm. "I worked in construction. The boss didn't like personal phone calls. Somebody called me off the backhoe. Said my wife was on the phone."

Tex paused and took a deep breath.

"Went to the office. The boss said to make it quick. I asked her what was wrong. Cassie said she was feeling poorly, and to come right home."

He paused and angrily wiped tears from his face.

"I said I was busy, and it'd have to wait 'til I got home. I hung up. When I got home, she lay dead on the floor, the phone by her hand."

Good lord! I rummaged through my purse for a tissue.

"I didn't know at the time, but she died right there. My last words to my wife of twenty years were that I was too busy for her."

Dropping his head into crossed arms, he repeated, "I'll never forgive myself. I'll never forgive…"

"Dear God, Tex, you have been suffering so much," I blurted.

Suddenly, I felt Rick's presence, and my words poured out, "When I landed in Heaven, I loved it! I felt totally furious when they made me leave. It must have been her time to go, Tex. She's at peace now and so happy. She's not mad at you, just saving you a place. It's all OK! I promise you!"

He sniffed, straightened up, and wiped his nose on his sleeve. "Are you sure?" he asked. "I can't go on living with this pain."

"Positive. I know she's forgiven you and loves you," I answered and added, "May I give you a hug?"

Tex edged off his seat and looked directly into my eyes, saying, "You're an angel, aren't ya? I used to watch that television show. You don't know it, but you saved my life here today. You've got to be an angel."

Then he leaned over to envelop me in a tight embrace and rocked me back and forth. Flattered, but uncomfortable at his effusive gesture, I eased from his arms and pulled my bag from under the counter. "I'd better go check on my flight," I said and started toward the door.

Tex's multiple beers caused his voice to be louder than the crowd noise as he repeatedly pointed at me, "This here lady is an angel, no foolin'! An angel, I tell you. Right here!"

Blending with the masses, I chuckled at my new nickname—better than "new kid," better than "tourist," I had somehow graduated to "angel," and I loved it!

For the first time since my expatriation from heaven, I felt certain I'd been sent back for a purpose. This changed everything for me: my outlook on life and the hope for a meaningful future.

I looked forward to more interactions with "my people," the ones on my invisible list of "too much left to do."

In the twenty years since my banishment, I've chalked up scores of mostly small opportunities to be kind and helpful. What pleasure and a sense of well-being fills me each time someone tells me, "I don't know what I'd have done if I hadn't run into you today" or "Thanks, I really needed to hear that."

I've flown a lot over the last five years, and many of my interactions occurred on airplanes. The first clue of an upcoming close encounter with one of "my people" is spotting them in the waiting room at the airport. They just catch my eye with an overheard conversation or incident of some kind.

Nine times out of ten, they end up sitting right next to me. I chuckle when spotting them come my way down the aisle, checking for seat numbers, and then plop down and say, "Hi!"

I've learned to close down my Kindle then, or put the airline magazine away, and just be available for their eventual introduction and sharing. It's actually quite fun!

It's not that I'm special. We all have the same task of being loving and kind to others, and ourselves, in this life. I guess I needed a jumpstart to open my eyes and heart to the reality of our common flawed existence and to what our loving God has planned for us.

The Message

One morning, as I gazed at the picture of Jesus I keep on my bedside table, I asked God what I needed to do to never go to hell again. How could I go to heaven instead?

I heard my Voice very clearly repeating: *Loving and kind, loving and kind, loving and kind.*

Still looking at Jesus, I asked the Voice what this meant.

It repeated the phrase and added several more words in quick succession. Confused, I asked again for clarification and mumbled aloud that I couldn't remember such a long list of words.

Since my illness, my memory has deteriorated, but the words *loving and kind* continued to echo intermittently.

And so began my new path to heaven via simple words.

For the next few days, the insistent message continued. I even espied the words combined on signs or in books and heard them in conversations. My new morning mantra was easy to remember, *"Jesus, help me to be loving and kind."*

A few months later, as I looked at His picture, I heard the words "merciful and forgiving." These were added to my morning meditation. A pattern was developing. When I heard the new words, a resonance occurred, and gently reminded me I needed work in that area of my life.

Two more words came to me later that year: "encouraging and grateful." Strangely, I found my adding the words proved easy. No memory problems with them whatsoever. In fact, the elongating phrase appeared seared into my brain. I could rattle off the list at will without a stutter.

After another long period, I was told, "Nonjudgmental." Ouch! This reminder came at a particularly relevant time.

A few months ago, one last word was shared with me. I was told to be "useful."

As I puzzled at the message, it dawned on me. It was time to write this book.

With seventy-three years behind me, I may be running out of time to fulfill my "too much left to do" assignment received at my former heaven check-out.

When people ask to hear my story, I always share these powerful words. If we are practicing these actions, we can't help but make the lives of others more joyful, thus becoming happier and more peaceful ourselves.

The second part of my avoidance of hell starts with a firm belief in my own jetting directly into God's realm after my next death, as so many other NDE experiencers did.

I've heard and read of the testaments of atheist and non-religious NDEers simply finding themselves in God's presence with no good/evil math prerequisite, but all returned believing their lives needed more interaction with God's directives of love and caring for others.

I choose to believe in God's unconditional and unparalleled love and mercy for me and await with as much confidence as my weak human self can muster for the incredible and overwhelming experience of being joined with God again and of finally being Home to stay.

Abridged Conclusion and Tip for Morning Prayer

God's answer to my question:

"What must I do to keep from going to hell again?"

"Be loving, kind, merciful, forgiving, encouraging, grateful, non-judgmental, and useful."

Epilogue

While resurrecting my deceased family's lives on paper, I often heard their spirits whispering in my ear. Sometimes, I awoke at some ungodly hour to hear a heavenly loved one reminding me of a story of events I'd long forgotten.

Once, an idea popped into my mind that my grandmother, Rachael, joined my life as a guiding spirit after her demise, and the two of us now work as a team trying to get it right this time. I found this idea comforting.

After a trip to hell and heaven, I have learned acceptance regarding unusual happenings and believe there are no coincidences, only events not fully understood.

Viewing my life as an experience I planned for myself removed any sense of victimhood. I try to integrate the lessons I chose to learn, instead of bemoaning my misfortune.

One of the worst things about hell, or hellish experiences on Earth, is the tendency to lose one's sense of humor.

If this precious accouterment is left to die on the battlefield, it can take a long time to restore. Armed with humor, we traverse this existence with a lighter step and put into perspective the direst of situations.

It's obvious God has a wonderful, sometimes zany, sense of humor, and we are made in His image. Thus, a loving and kind sense of humor is our birthright.

On a final note, as science continues to explore and edge toward acceptance of near-death experiences, it may soon be socially acceptable to view our participation in forever as a fact.

There is no "opt-out" box to check when you die, so please prepare thoughtfully.